More Nickel Quilts

20 New Designs from 5-Inch Squares

PAT SPETH

Martingale®
& COMPANY

DEDICATION

To my children–Ray, for being my Web master, for all his computer support, and for setting an example for reaching goals; and Roxie, for giving up an entire Thanksgiving break to work nonstop with me on the last two quilts for this book, and for her continued enthusiasm and support for whatever I do.

ACKNOWLEDGMENTS

I want to extend a special thank you to all the doctors and staff at Dentistry Unlimited for your encouragement and support during my career change. I also want to thank the members of the Mississippi Valley Quilt Guild and my fellow quilt retreaters for their friendship and enthusiasm for Nickel quilts. And last, I want to thank Martingale & Company for helping me reach my goals.

CREDITS

President	Nancy J. Martin
CEO	Daniel J. Martin
Publisher	Jane Hamada
Editorial Director	Mary V. Green
Managing Editor	Tina Cook
Technical Editor	Laurie Baker
Copy Editor	Ellen Balstad
Design Director	Stan Green
Illustrator	Laurel Strand
Cover and Text Designer	Regina Girard
Photographer	Brent Kane

That Patchwork Place® is an imprint of Martingale & Company®.

More Nickel Quilts:
20 New Designs from 5-Inch Squares
© 2004 by Pat Speth

Martingale & Company
20205 144th Avenue NE
Woodinville, WA 98072-8478 USA
www.martingale-pub.com

Printed in China
09 08 07   8 7 6 5

MISSION STATEMENT

Dedicated to providing quality products and service to inspire creativity.

Library of Congress Cataloging-in-Publication Data
Speth, Pat.
  More nickel quilts : 20 new designs from 5-inch squares / Pat Speth.
    p. cm.
  "That Patchwork Place."
  ISBN 978-1-56477-552-8
  1. Patchwork—Patterns. 2. Quilting—Patterns. I. Title.
  TT835 .S6525 2004
  746 .46 ' 041—dc22
                                    2004003591

Contents

Why Nickel Quilts?

I love scrappy quilts, and this method for making them with 5" squares is fast and easy. When Charlene Thode and I published *Nickel Quilts* (Martingale & Company, 2002), quilters everywhere began cutting their fabric stash into 5" squares. As the book's popularity increased, I thought I'd better put together another collection.

For those of you unfamiliar with the Nickel quilts method, this is how it works. First, you begin with a collection of "nickel" squares. What's a "nickel" square? It is a 5" square of quilting fabric. You'll need lots of them to make a scrappy Nickel quilt. Because gathering fabrics for a Nickel quilt can take time, I have developed a method for building your stash of 5" squares quickly through fabric trades with friends, new and old, who share your love for quilting.

Each of the quilt patterns in this book is rated by skill level—beginner, easy, or intermediate—based on the degree of piecing difficulty. If you're new to quilting, start with a beginner quilt. If you have some quilting experience, choose an easy project. Once you've used the easy unit construction methods to make your first Nickel quilt, you'll be ready to move on to one of the more challenging projects. Note that sometimes a quilt has an intermediate rating because of the pieced border; remember that you can make all the quilts with plain borders, and all of the border treatments can be used on other quilts besides Nickel quilts.

You will use combinations of eight different units to create the blocks used in the quilts featured in this book. The instructions for making the units begin on page 11. My simple method of sewing and dividing a 5" square into pieced units speeds up scrap quiltmaking. To really understand the process, it is essential to review the unit construction steps for each unit before you begin. It is also important to make a sample block or blocks for the quilt you are making. The information at the beginning of each project's "Making the Blocks" section will tell you what you need for making one block. This information is useful for planning the pieces to use in each block, as well as for determining what you will need if you want to add more blocks to your quilt top.

Once you learn the process, you'll be making scrap quilts faster than you ever dreamed possible!

–Pat

How to Gather 5" Squares

Maybe you're new to quilting and you haven't built up a stash of scraps yet, or maybe you just love fabric and want to add to your stash! Either way, this section will give you easy, inexpensive ways to build your collection.

START CUTTING

So, how do you start collecting all those 5" squares? Start by cutting strips from your own fabric collection. When fabric shopping, always buy a little more than you need for your project so that you can cut a 5"-wide strip from each one—after you've tested it for colorfastness, preshrunk it, and trimmed away the selvages. Cut each strip into squares and store for future use. You'll be surprised how quickly your pile grows with your fabric purchases alone.

Want to make the variety in your collection of squares grow even faster? Plan a cutting bee with a few friends and swap strips. In addition, many quilt shops and mail-order catalogs offer packets of 5" squares. Don't forget to check out all those new Internet fabric shopping sites, too. Not only can you buy fabric packets online, but there are also dozens of online groups of quilters interested in fabric trades. Fat-quarter trades are wonderful. Did you know you can cut twelve 5" squares from one fat quarter? Use some in your current scrap project and put the leftovers away for another quilt.

If you aren't able to access the Internet, look through your quilting magazines for postings from quilters who want to participate in fabric trades—or you can post a message yourself, asking for fabric trading partners. When you trade with others from different states and countries, your selection of squares becomes that much more varied and unique. If staying a bit closer to home is more your style, then start a trade with your local quilt guild or your smaller "sit-and-sew" group.

A FEW TRADING GUIDELINES

You may find it helpful to have a few guidelines for organizing a fabric trade. Begin by enlisting a friend or two to help out.

- Select the type(s) of fabric the group would like to trade. For example, you could begin by designating a color, or a type of print, such as stripes, stars, paisleys, florals, or plaids. Or, you could decide to swap fabrics that represent specific time periods—1800s or 1930s reproduction fabrics, for example. Some swappers even go so far as to designate the manufacturers whose fabrics they want to swap (this is great for quality control).

- Decide how many times per year you want to trade. If you're trading with guild members, you could schedule six trades per year so participants can drop off packets one month and pick them up the next. Midway between your regular meetings, get a small group of volunteers together to organize the fabric into sets for pickup. Those who may have missed the drop-off meeting can still participate at that time if they drop off their fabric.

- Determine how many squares you're going to trade. That number will depend a lot on the size of your group. You may want to ask people to sign up first to get an idea of the number of participants you'll have. Be sure to let them know that they can submit multiple trades. As an example, in my guild each person brings 72 squares, or 36 pairs, for one trade, and as long as there are at least 36 trades turned in, no one receives any duplicates. I've discovered that trading the 5" squares of fabric in pairs makes it easier to create a wider range of blocks and frees up the design elements of your quilts. It is also faster and easier to lift a pair of squares off of a pile rather than trying to separate one square at a time.

- Make sure everyone understands that *all fabrics must be 100% cotton* and that they must be *preshrunk and tested for colorfastness* before the swap. Selvages must be removed before you cut the strips.

Nickel Tip

I add a piece of muslin when washing my fabrics, especially reds and other dark colors. If the muslin turns color, I have a fabric that is bleeding.

- Remind all participants to trade fabrics they would like to receive. Depending on who is involved, the fabrics you receive might not be ones you would have personally selected—but that's what makes scrap quilts so interesting.

- Ask participants to stack their trade in twos, turning every other pair of 5" squares an eighth turn. This makes lifting the pairs of squares off the pile go much faster. Place them in a gallon-size plastic bag with the participant's name on the outside.

- Plan a party! Pick a day to get together and trade the fabrics. Think about having a potluck lunch or dessert party. Most important, have *fun*. Remember, anyone who comes to help with the swap gets to fondle the fabric first! It's nice to have a large space for setting out the trades. Ping-Pong tables are great. Count the number of trades turned in and mark as many places on the table with slips of paper. Beginning at one end, place one pair of fabrics on each slip of paper. When the first stack runs out, start on the next stack and keep going until all of the fabrics have been traded. Place one traded stack back into each reusable bag to take back to the next meeting.

Once you have a wonderful stack of 5" squares, half the work—the cutting—is already done! Just select the squares for your blocks and start sewing. Once you see what a big time-saver this method is, you'll be wishing you'd started trading a long time ago.

5"-Square Yardage Yield

(Based on 40" of usable width after preshrinking)

¼ yard = 8 squares
1 fat quarter = 12 squares
½ yard = 24 squares
¾ yard = 40 squares
1 yard = 56 squares

WHAT ABOUT OTHER SIZES?

If you have been trading something other than 5" squares, don't worry. The alternate square chart below gives the unfinished size of the various units you can make for the quilts in this book. (The 5" square unit dimensions are included for your reference.) You can follow the same methods in the unit construction section but just be aware that because the block size will be different, the measurements in the illustrations will not match your unit measurements. You will also need to recalculate the yardage for sashings, borders, and backing when you substitute squares of a different size.

ALTERNATE SQUARE CHART

Unit	4" Square	5" Square	6" Square
Large two-patch	3½" x 3½"	4½" x 4½"	5½" x 5½"
Small two-patch	2" x 3½"	2½" x 4½"	3" x 5½"
Four-patch	3½" x 3½"	4½" x 4½"	5½" x 5½"
Half-square-triangle	3½" x 3½"	4½" x 4½"	5½" x 5½"
Small-wonders	1¾" x 1¾"	2¼" x 2¼"	2¾" x 2¾"
Combination	3¼" x 3¼"	4¼" x 4¼"	5¼" x 5¼"
Hourglass	3" x 3"	4" x 4"	5" x 5"
Picket-fence	2" x 3½"	2½" x 4½"	3" x 5½"
Flying-geese	2" x 3½"	2½" x 4½"	3" x 5½"

General Instructions

Look to this section for the basic tools and techniques used to make the quilts. Chances are, if you've got scraps, you'll already have everything you need on hand.

TAKING STOCK OF YOUR SEWING TOOLS

Before you start your first Nickel quilt, make sure you have the following basic tools:

B.S.K. (that's Basic Sewing Kit): My B.S.K. consists of thread, a small pair of scissors, a tool to help guide the fabric under the presser foot (perhaps a seam ripper or stiletto), pins, needles, measuring tape, bandages (for the occasional rotary-cutting accident), a mechanical pencil and small notebook for making notes and keeping track of all the new ideas that I get while sewing, and a seam ripper.

Design wall: You'll need—and want—a design wall. My design wall is portable and fits into my car so that I can take it along to retreats and workshops. See the box at right to make your own portable design wall.

Iron and ironing surface: You can use a tabletop ironing surface when constructing and pressing the units, but you will definitely need a full-size ironing board or other large pressing surface as your quilt grows and you add the borders.

Rotary cutter and mat: I work with two sizes of mats—one large enough to accommodate the fabric when folded in half with the selvages aligned and a smaller mat to keep next to the sewing machine for trimming pieced units during construction. I also work only with sharp rotary cutters in different sizes. I use the small size for trimming units and the medium and larger sizes for cutting 5" squares and border fabrics. To avoid frustration, don't put off changing the blade on the rotary cutter when it dulls or develops "skips" when cutting. Using a dull blade doubles your work, and quilt-making is about having fun, not about getting frustrated with your cutter.

Rulers: You'll need a 6" or larger square ruler with a 45° angle marked, and a 6" x 24" ruler for cutting.

Sewing machine: Make sure your sewing machine is in good working order! Give it a good cleaning and put in a new needle. I recommend changing the machine needle at the beginning of a new project or after approximately ten to fifteen hours of actual sewing time.

Portable Design Wall

In less than five minutes and with only a few easy-to-find materials, you can make an inexpensive and portable design wall that you can take anywhere and that doesn't take a lot of storage space when not in use.

- 1 dressmaker's cardboard cutting board (the kind that folds up for storage)
- 2 strips of 1" x 2" wood, each at least 5' long; they can be longer, but just be sure they will fit in your vehicle and aren't taller than your sewing-room ceilings
- A 40" x 72" piece of white flannel or a flannel-backed vinyl tablecloth
- 6 large binder clips (from an office-supply store)

1. Unfold the cutting board and place it on a flat surface.
2. Place the wood strips underneath along the long edges of the cutting board, making sure they are even across the bottom so that the design wall sits squarely on the floor.
3. Lay the flannel on top of the cutting board and fasten the three layers—wood, cutting board, and flannel—together with binder clips. Use three clips on each long edge.

SELECTING FABRIC AND THREAD

I recommend buying good-quality, 100%-cotton fabrics and threads. Use a neutral color thread for piecing scrap quilts. Tan, gray, and off-white are all good choices because they blend with the wide assortment of colors in the varied fabrics you'll be using in your scrap quilts. Use the same kind of thread on top and in the bobbin for piecing and for machine quilting. This strategy prevents a lot of sewing-machine "tension" headaches.

Many of the quilts in this book have a very definite theme reflected in the colors and fabrics I chose, but most of them would look great in other fabric types too. Choose colors to suit your taste. Emphasize color value and vary the size of print motifs in the fabric assortment for a quilt. When selecting fabrics for the borders, consider whether a pieced border is involved. For borders that surround a pieced border, I use a tone-on-tone fabric or a fabric that "reads" as a solid from a distance. Any fabric with too much texture will distract from the pieced border and will look too busy. For plain borders in quilts, I use anything from a busy small print to a showy large-scale print.

The Value of Value

Because the quilts in this book are all scrappy and each is made from lots of different fabrics, it's more important to pay attention to the value of the fabrics (whether they are light, medium, or dark) than it is to worry about how they relate to each other on the color wheel. If you plan the placement of dark-, medium-, and light-colored fabrics correctly within the blocks and evenly distribute the various colors you've used throughout the quilt top, you'll achieve the same effect without obsessing about it.

If you're confused about whether a fabric is dark, medium, or light, try separating your fabrics into a dark pile and a light pile. You'll soon realize that you have a few that aren't either one; those are the mediums. Just be aware that a medium fabric can look dark next to a white fabric or a light tone-on-tone print but light next to a very dark blue or black fabric.

For an inexpensive value finder, purchase a red plastic report cover (available at your local office-supply store) and view your fabrics through it. You won't be able to see the actual colors of the fabric through the red plastic—just the values. Test this technique with fabrics from your scrap bag. Experimenting is the best way to learn.

NOTE: The red plastic value finder does not work with red fabrics, but if you get proficient at identifying value in other colors, you'll find it fairly easy to judge red values, too.

The Value of Variety

When choosing fabrics for a scrap quilt, it's important to vary the size of the prints, stripes, or plaids. Be sure you mix in large floral prints with small geometrics and large plaids with stripes. Throw in a few holiday or novelty fabrics as well. Using a variety of background fabrics in the blocks rather than just one can be fun also. It adds more interest and movement to the finished quilt. If, however, the main fabrics you are working with are busy or large prints, you might want to stay with one background fabric to calm the prints down. I actually have used the wrong side of fabrics for backgrounds to get the results I want.

PREPARING THE FABRIC

I am definitely in favor of prewashing all fabrics. In fact, all of the fabric trades I participate in require prewashing. Using prewashed fabrics helps reduce the likelihood of having a fabric bleed or run later and ruin all your hard work. In addition, a quilt top made with both washed and unwashed fabrics is more likely to shrink unevenly, leaving unsightly puckers in the laundered quilt. Remember to add a piece of muslin to the wash load of fabrics to test for colorfastness.

To prevent wrinkles from setting, avoid letting your fabrics sit in the dryer for any great length of time after they are dry. Wrinkles make ironing the fabrics a real job.

When it comes time to wash your finished quilt, I recommend that you wash it with a very mild soap or one developed specifically for cleaning quilts. I use Orvus paste to launder my finished quilts.

CUTTING THE STRIPS AND SQUARES

After you've prepared your fabric, it's time to cut it into strips and squares. Choose your fabric squares and make a sample block before cutting all of the fabrics for your quilt project. You will learn and practice the steps required to make the block, which will allow you to speed up the piecing. You can also check and adjust color and value placement if necessary.

1. Straighten the fabric. Hold it in front of you with the selvages aligned and examine the fold. If there are waves or wrinkles along the folded edge, realign the selvages to the right or left until the fold is hanging evenly. Don't worry about the cut edges (crosswise grain) of the fabric. Even if you've torn the fabric instead of cutting it, this edge may still be off when you align the selvages so that *the folded edge is smooth and flat.* Place the fabric on the cutting mat with the folded edge along one of the grid lines on the mat.

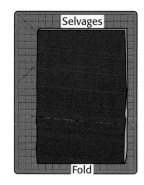

Selvages

Fold

2. To make the first cut, place the ruler along the folded edge and align a crosswise line with the fold. Cut the strip slightly wider than the actual size you need. For example, if you need a 5"-wide strip, be sure to cut it at least 5½" wide to begin. Hold the rotary cutter against the ruler and cut alongside it, moving the cutter away from your body. Stop and move the hand that's holding the ruler as needed to keep the ruler from slipping out of position.

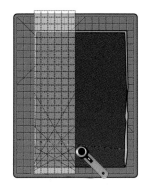

3. Turn the entire mat around and trim the strip to the correct width, cutting the excess off of the uneven edge. Try not to disturb the rest of the fabric during this process. Turn the mat around again and continue cutting the required amount of strips in *the width needed.* Only the first strip needs to be cut wider than necessary.

4. Cut the strips into squares. A method I use allows me to cut several strips at one time. Position a fabric strip on the mat with one long edge along one of the horizontal grid lines. Align the selvage edge with a vertical grid line. Place the next strip of fabric on top of the first one, but move it up one grid line. The selvages of the second strip should be along the same vertical grid line as the first strip. Continue to layer up to five strips of fabric in this way. (To ensure accurate cuts, don't try to layer more than five layers, and make sure you have a nice sharp rotary blade.)

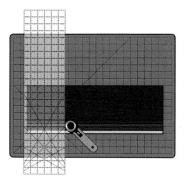

Layer strips before cutting squares.

5. Make the first cut as you did when cutting the strips. Position the ruler on the fabric, aligning the markings along the top and bottom edges of the fabric strips. Make sure that the first cut allows for a wider strip than required so that there is room to trim away the selvages. Putting pressure on both the ruler and the rotary cutter, make the first cut. Turn the mat around to trim the selvages from the first cut.

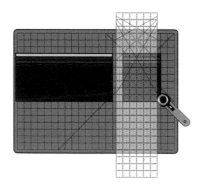

Trim selvages from first cut.

6. Turn the mat back around, align the ruler at the top and bottom edges, and cut the remainder of the strips into squares.

SEWING, PINNING, AND MARKING

All of the quilts in this book are made using ¼"-wide seam allowances. If you have a ¼" presser foot for your machine, use it to stitch accurate seam widths. If you don't, measure ¼" from the point of the needle to the right and mark the bed of your machine with a strip of masking tape or a piece of padded moleskin (a foot-care product, available at your local drug store). Padded moleskin is thicker than tape and creates a raised guide for the fabric edges while you are stitching.

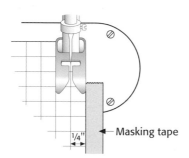

1/4" ← Masking tape

In some cases, I will tell you to use a "slim" ¼"-wide seam allowance. This means that you will stitch a slightly narrower seam so that the stitching is a thread from the normal ¼" seam line. This allows for the thickness of the sewing thread in the seam allowance and actually results in a more accurately sized unit.

In other cases, you will be instructed to stitch a "very slim" ¼"-wide seam. In these instances, use a ³⁄₁₆"-wide seam allowance. This ensures that all of the pieces are accurate where it takes several seams to complete a unit.

Chain Sewing

Chain sewing is a great way to save time and thread. Simply stitch two pieces together, stitch off the end of the pieces, and feed the next set of pieces under the foot without clipping the thread. This will also help keep the pieces in order when you join the rows in the blocks.

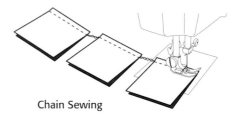

Chain Sewing

To Pin or Not to Pin

That is the question. It depends on you and your sewing machine. I recommend pinning when points need to be matched, when you are sewing on bias edges, and when joining blocks and adding borders. Use pins that have a fine shaft to avoid damaging the fabric. Fine pins also slide in and out of fabric more easily. Place pins approximately every two inches. Don't ever sew over the pins; remove them before you reach them to avoid snagged fabric, bent pins, and broken needles.

Marking

I mark the stitching line on the picket-fence and flying-geese units. I have tried a variety of methods for sewing these units without marking the actual stitching line, but I find that I have the most accurate results when the line is marked. Of course, you are free to use another method for these units if you prefer.

CONSTRUCTING AND PRESSING UNITS

The quilts in this book are made from combinations of eight different units: two-patch, four-patch, half-square-triangle, small-wonders, combination, hour-glass, picket-fence, and flying-geese. Follow the instructions shown below to construct the various units. Be sure to "set the seams" by placing the iron on the stitched seam line before pressing it to one side. Remember: *press; do not iron.*

Two-Patch Units

There are two different sizes of two-patch units—small and large.

To make small two-patch units:

1. With right sides together, place a 5" square of the background fabric on a 5" square of the main fabric. Stitch ¼"-wide seams on opposite sides of the unit. Cut the unit in half so that each piece measures 2½" x 5".

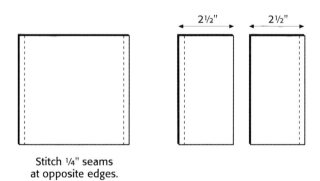

Stitch ¼" seams
at opposite edges.

2. Press to set the stitching; then press the seams toward the darker fabric in each unit.

Press.

3. Cut each pressed unit in half across the seam as shown so that each of the four resulting two-patch units measures 2½" x 4½".

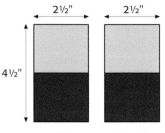

Small Two-Patch Units

To make large two-patch units:

1. Follow steps 1 and 2 for small two-patch units.

2. Trim ½" from one edge of each of the two resulting units as shown so that each unit measures 4½" square.

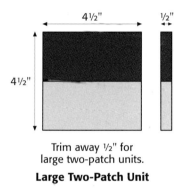

Trim away ½" for
large two-patch units.

Large Two-Patch Unit

Four-Patch Units

1. Follow steps 1 and 2 for small two-patch units.

2. Place two units right sides together with seams aligned horizontally and the dark and light fabrics opposite each other; stitch ¼"-wide seams on opposite sides of the unit. Be sure the stitching crosses the first seam. Cut the resulting unit in half.

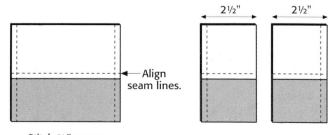

Align
seam lines.

Stitch ¼" seams
at opposite edges.

NOTE: To make "scrappy" four-patch units, simply use units that have different fabrics in them and continue on with step 3.

3. Press to set the stitching; then press the seam to one side in each of the two resulting four-patch units.

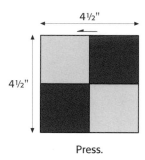

Press.

Four-Patch Unit

Half-Square-Triangle Units

1. Draw a diagonal line on the wrong side of a 5" square of background fabric. With right sides together, place the marked background square on top of a square of the main fabric.

Wrong side of background fabric

2. Stitch a "slim" ¼"-wide seam on both sides of the diagonal line (refer to "Sewing, Pinning, and Marking" on page 10).

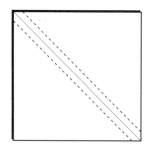

Stitch a "slim" ¼"
on each side of the line.

3. Cut along the diagonal line to yield two half-square-triangle units.

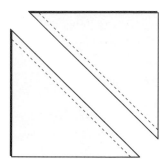

Cut on the diagonal line.

4. Press to set the stitching; then press the seam in each unit toward the dark fabric, unless otherwise instructed in the individual block illustrations for the quilt you are making.

Press.

5. To trim the units, place the 45° diagonal line of your square ruler along the seam line. Position it so that the fabric extends past the ruler on two adjacent sides, and the remaining sides extend past the 4½" lines on the ruler. Trim away the fabric that extends beyond the ruler edges.

45°
line

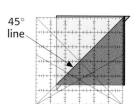 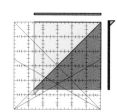

Trim excess.

6. Reposition the unit so that the two trimmed edges now line up along the 4½" lines on the ruler and the 45° diagonal line is along the seam line. Trim the remaining two edges for a perfect 4½" half-square-triangle unit.

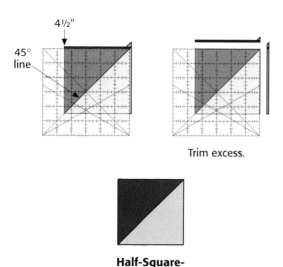

Trim excess.

Half-Square-Triangle Unit

Small-Wonders Units

1. Follow steps 1–6 of "Half-Square-Triangle Units" on page 12 to make a half-square-triangle unit. Cut the unit in half as shown.

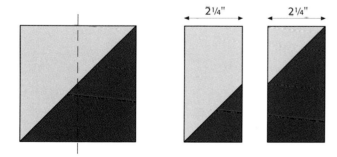

2. Lift the ruler carefully and reposition it so the 2¼" line is along the lower edge of the units. Cut along the upper edge of the ruler. You should have four different pieces, each one measuring 2¼" square.

The pieces will be stitched together in different arrangements depending on the quilt design.

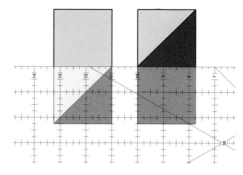

Position 2¼" line at lower edge of units.

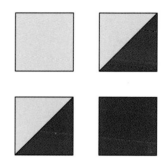

Each unit should measure 2¼" square.
Small-Wonders Units

Combination Units

1. For this unit only, use a "very slim" ¼"-wide seam allowance (refer to "Sewing, Pinning, and Marking" on page 10), and follow steps 1–4 of "Half-Square-Triangle Units" on page 12 to make a half-square-triangle unit. *Do not trim the unit.*

2. On the wrong side of the untrimmed half-square-triangle unit, draw a diagonal line perpendicular to the seam line.

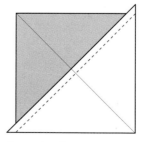

Untrimmed Half-Square-Triangle Unit

3. With right sides together, center the marked unit on top of a 5" square of fabric. (The marked unit will be slightly smaller than the 5" square.) Stitch a "very slim" seam on both sides of the diagonal line.

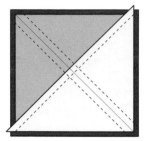

Stitch a "very slim" ¼" seam
on each side of diagonal line.

4. Cut on the diagonal line to yield a right-sided and left-sided unit. Press to set the stitching; then press the seam toward the large triangle in each unit.

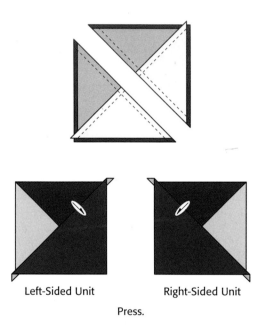

Left-Sided Unit   Right-Sided Unit
Press.

5. To trim each unit, align the 45° diagonal line of the square ruler with the long seam line. Position the ruler so that the fabric extends past the ruler on two adjacent edges, with the two remaining edges extending past the 4¼" lines of the ruler and with

the 4¼" line meeting the short seam line on the unit. Trim away the fabric extending past the ruler.

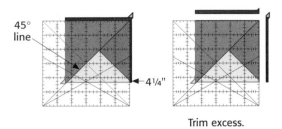

Trim excess.

6. Reposition the unit so that the two trimmed edges now line up with the 4¼" lines on the ruler, and the 45° diagonal line of the ruler is aligned with the long diagonal seam line. Trim the remaining two edges. You should have a perfect, 4¼"-square combination unit.

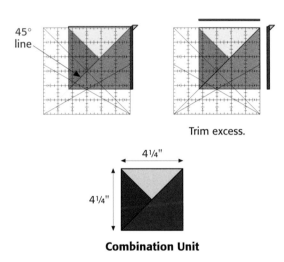

Trim excess.

Combination Unit

Hourglass Units

1. Follow steps 1–4 of "Half-Square-Triangle Units" on page 12 to make two half-square-triangle units. *Do not trim the units.* On the wrong side of one untrimmed half-square-triangle unit, draw a diagonal line perpendicular to the seam line.

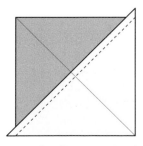

Untrimmed Half-Square-Triangle Unit

2. With right sides together and the dark and light triangles opposite each other, place the marked unit on top of the second half-square-triangle unit. Stitch a "slim" ¼" seam on both sides of the diagonal line (refer to "Sewing, Pinning, and Marking" on page 10).

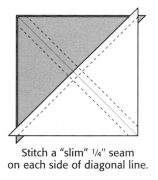

Stitch a "slim" ¼" seam
on each side of diagonal line.

3. Cut on the diagonal line to yield two hourglass units.

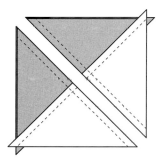

4. Press to set the stitching; then press the seam to one side in each unit.

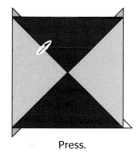

Press.

5. To trim each unit, align the 45° diagonal line of the ruler along one of the seam lines. Position the ruler so that the fabric extends past the ruler on two adjacent sides and the remaining two sides extend past the 4" lines of the ruler, with the 4" lines meeting the seam lines at the top left and bottom right of the unit. Trim away the fabric that extends past the ruler.

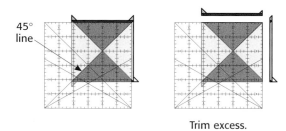

Trim excess.

6. Reposition the unit so that the two trimmed edges line up with the 4" lines on the ruler and the diagonal ruler line is aligned with the diagonal seam line. Trim away the remaining two edges. You should have a perfect, 4"-square hourglass unit.

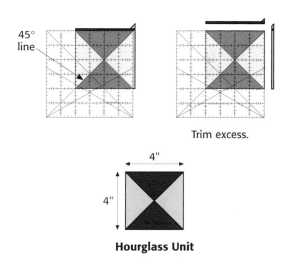

Trim excess.

Hourglass Unit

Picket-Fence Units

1. Trim away ½" from one edge of a 5" square.

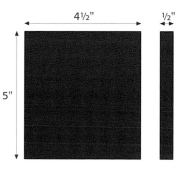

Trim ½" from one edge.

Sew and Flip

Both the flying-geese and picket-fence units utilize the "sew-and-flip" method to add the small squares that become the triangular corners after trimming. *When adding these units, stitch one thread width to the outside of the diagonal line.* This stitching strategy allows for the thickness of the thread in the seam and results in a more accurately sized block after pressing.

Waste Triangles

Waste triangles are "bonus" half-square triangles that you can make when constructing picket-fence and flying-geese units by using the corners that are cut away. Sew the small squares in place as directed, and then stitch again ½" from the first line of stitching. You can "eyeball" this seam because you will trim these small half-square-triangle units to the exact size you need when you use them in a future project. Lightly press to set the stitching, and then

cut between the two lines of stitching. For free waste-triangle projects, visit www.patspeth.com.

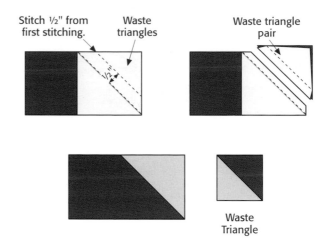

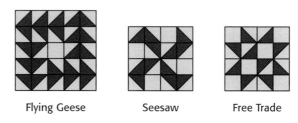

Following are just a few examples of blocks made using waste triangles.

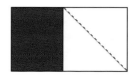

Flying Geese   Seesaw   Free Trade

2. Cut the trimmed piece in half *in the opposite direction of the first cut* so that the two resulting pieces each measure 2½" x 4½".

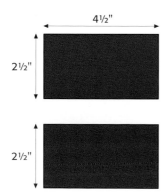

3. Draw a diagonal line on the wrong side of a 2½" square of background fabric. With right sides together, place this 2½" square on top of a 2½" x 4½" rectangle at the right-hand end. Stitch one thread width to the outside of the diagonal line. Chain sew (see page 10) several of these at a time. If you want to save the waste triangles for other projects, refer to the instructions above.

Stitch one thread to the outside
of the diagonal line.

4. Lightly press to set the stitching; then press the seam toward the small triangle, unless otherwise directed in the individual block illustrations for the quilt you are making. Check the alignment of the triangle with the edge of the rectangle.

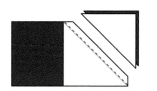

Check alignment of triangle and rectangle edges.

Press.

5. Fold back the edge of the 2½" square and cut ¼" from the stitching line. Press the triangle back into place.

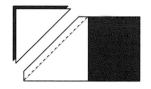

Press.
Picket-Fence Unit

6. For a mirror-image pair of picket-fence units, repeat steps 1–5 at the left-hand end of a rectangle.

Picket-Fence Unit
(Mirror-Image)

Flying-Geese Units

1. Choose 5" squares for the center triangles in the flying-geese units and trim ½" from one edge.

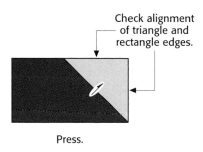

4½"   ½"

5"

Trim ½" from one edge.

2. Repeat steps 2–5 for picket-fence units to cut the trimmed piece in half and sew a 2½" background square to the right-hand edge of each rectangle. Repeat to add a background square to the left-hand edge of each rectangle. Each flying-geese unit should measure 2½" x 4½".

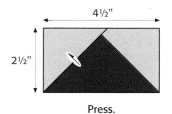

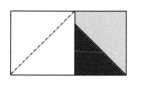

4½"

2½"

Press.
Flying-Geese Unit

Finishing Your Quilt

Once your blocks are finished, it's time to stitch them together, add borders, and finish your quilt. This section will cover all the necessary details for completing your project.

ASSEMBLING THE QUILT TOP

You can stitch your blocks together in either a straight or on-point (diagonal) setting. For straight sets, join the blocks in horizontal rows, pressing seams in opposite directions from row to row. Sew the completed rows together.

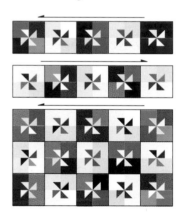

Straight-Set Quilt

To set blocks on point, arrange and sew the blocks and setting triangles together in diagonal rows before joining the rows and adding corner triangles to complete the quilt top. Using a design wall to arrange the blocks for either type of setting arrangement is very helpful, especially for on-point settings.

Unless the setting includes sashing strips between the blocks, press the seams in opposite directions from row to row. This helps the seam intersections nestle together for perfectly matched seams in the finished quilt top. When sashing strips and squares are used in a quilt setting, press all seams toward the sashing pieces.

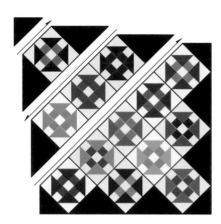

Diagonally Set Quilt

ADDING THE BORDERS

For the quilts in this book, you will add either plain borders or pieced borders combined with plain inner and outer borders to complete your quilt top.

Plain Borders

1. To determine the cut length of the side-border strips, measure the length of the quilt top through the center. Cut two border strips to this length.

2. Fold each strip in half and then in half again and mark the quarter-points at the fold with pins. Fold and pin mark the side edges of the quilt top in the same manner.

3. With right sides together and marking pins aligned, pin the border strips to the quilt top. Stitch ¼" from the raw edges to attach each border.

4. Press to set the stitching; then press the seam toward the border.

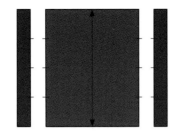

Measure center of quilt, top to bottom.
Mark centers and quarter marks.

5. Measure the width of the quilt top through the center, including the borders you just added. Cut the top and bottom border strips to match this measurement. Pin mark the borders and the quilt top as you did for the side borders. Pin, stitch, and press.

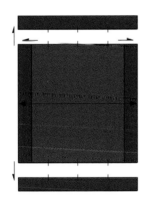

Measure center of quilt,
side to side, including borders.
Mark centers and quarter marks.

6. If your quilt has multiple plain borders, repeat steps 1–5 to attach each additional border.

Pieced Borders

Whenever a quilt in this book has pieced borders, it also has an inner or "spacer" border and an outer plain border.

NOTE: The cut width for the inner borders as given in the cutting table for each quilt is correct, *but only if all of your seams were 100% accurate throughout the block and quilt-top assembly. It is best to wait and cut the inner borders after the blocks have been joined to create the quilt top.*

1. Measure the length and width of the quilt top through the center and subtract ½" from each dimension for seam allowances.

2. Measure the length of the top and bottom pieced borders. Subtract the finished size of the two corner units plus ½" for seam allowances from each pieced-border measurement. Measure the length of the side-border strips. Subtract ½" for seam allowances.

3. Compare the measurements of the top and bottom pieced-border strips. *If they are not the same, you must adjust them so that they are before you go any further.* To adjust them, take in or let out seam allowances to make them equal. Repeat to compare the side-border strip measurements and adjust them if necessary.

4. Use the formula as shown in the following examples to determine the cut width for the inner-border strips.

Length of top and bottom pieced borders (step 2 above)	**80"** (a)
Subtract width of quilt top (step 1 above)	- **75"** (b) = **5"** (c)
Divide (c) by 2	= **2.5"** (d)
Add ½" for seam allowances	+ **.5"** = **3"** cut width for side inner-border strips
Length of side pieced borders (step 2 above)	**90"** (e)
Subtract length of quilt top (step 1 above)	- **87"** (f) = **3"** (g)
Divide (g) by 2	= **1.5"** (h)
Add ½" for seam allowances	+ **.5"** = **2"** cut width for top and bottom inner-border strips

NOTE: In case you're wondering if I've made a mistake, it is true that in some cases the top and bottom inner-border strips will not be the same width as the side inner-border strips.

After you have determined the strip width for the inner borders, add all borders, referring to the instructions for "Plain Borders" on page 18.

MARKING THE QUILT TOP FOR QUILTING

If you have a specific quilting design in mind, mark the quilt top *before* you baste the layers together. (I quilt most of my quilts on a long-arm machine in a meandering design that doesn't need to be marked). Test the marking tool you choose on a scrap of fabric to be sure you can remove it later.

MAKING THE QUILT BACKING

It is usually necessary to piece the backing for a quilt. To make sure you use the backing yardage correctly (so you don't run short), choose the illustration below that most closely matches the quilt-top dimensions. Cut the yardage into the required number of pieces.

Because selvages shrink at a different rate than the remainder of the quilt and can cause the backing seams to pucker, *it is important to remove all selvages from the backing fabric before piecing the backing.*

The measurements shown below allow for an additional 2" of backing on each side of the quilt. If you are going to have your quilt professionally quilted, you will want to add at least another 2" on each side.

Quilts Up to 80" Long

Quilts Over 80" Long and Less Than 80" wide

Quilts Over 80" Wide

LAYERING, BASTING, AND QUILTING

You are ready to make a "quilt sandwich" with the backing, batting, and quilt top.

1. Place the backing facedown on a large, smooth, flat surface—a large table or two pushed together, or on the floor. Smooth out any wrinkles and use masking tape to secure the backing to the surface. Make sure it is on grain and taut.

Nickel Tip

If you are layering your quilt on a carpeted floor, use large "T" pins to pin the backing to the carpet and pad.

2. Arrange the batting on top of the backing and smooth it into place.

Nickel Tip

If you have purchased a packaged batting, you need to let it relax or breathe. Lay it out over a bed overnight. If you are like me, however, and tend to forget, toss it in the dryer on the air or fluff cycle.

3. Place the quilt top, face up, on top of the batting.
4. Pin or thread baste the layers together. For pin basting, place pins approximately every 4" to 6" starting in the center of the quilt and working out to the edges. If you are thread basting, begin in the center of the quilt and work out in opposite directions, first toward the top, and then toward the bottom, through the center of the quilt. Use large stitches for this—and space them at least 2" apart. Next, start in the center again and work to the right and left. Continue in this manner until the entire top is basted in a grid, with stitched lines spaced approximately 4" to 5" apart. It's a good idea to baste diagonally across the quilt in both directions too.

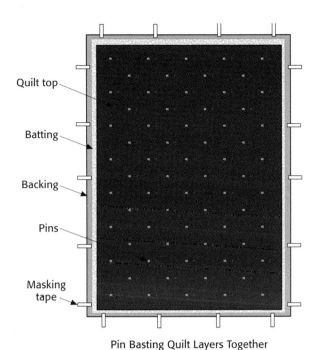

Quilt top

Batting

Backing

Pins

Masking tape

Pin Basting Quilt Layers Together

5. Hand or machine quilt as desired.

6. At this point you can trim the excess batting and backing even with the quilt-top edges, making sure all the corners are square. Or, you can wait to trim until after the binding is stitched to the quilt top and before it is stitched to the backing.

ADDING THE BINDING

Good work! You're almost done. It's time to add the binding. I used a straight-grain, French (double-layer) binding for all the quilts in this book.

1. Sew the binding strips together to create one long piece. Use bias seams as shown and press all seams open.

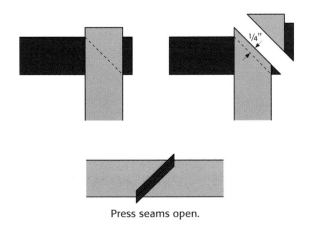

Press seams open.

2. Press the binding strip in half lengthwise with wrong sides together and raw edges even.

3. If available, attach a walking foot or engage the even-feed feature on your machine. Beginning in the center on one of the sides and leaving the first 10" of the binding free from the stitching, stitch ¼" from the raw edges. Stitch to the corner of the quilt, stopping ¼" from the raw edge, and backstitch two stitches. Clip the threads.

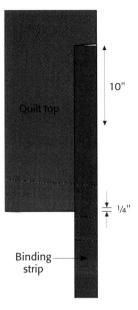

Quilt top

10"

¼"

Binding strip

4. Remove the quilt from the machine and rotate it ¼ turn to the left. Fold the binding strip up and away from the quilt, forming a 45°-angle fold at the corner. Holding the fold in place with a pin, fold the binding back onto the quilt to form a fold parallel to and even with the quilt-top raw edge.

5. With raw edges of the binding even with the quilt edges, stitch ¼" from the fold, backstitching to secure the end. Continue around the remaining sides of the quilt in the same manner, stopping approximately 12" from where you started stitching.

6. Now you are ready to join the binding ends. Position the raw edges of the beginning end of the binding even with the quilt raw edges. Lap the end of the binding strip over the beginning of the binding strip. Leaving a 2½" overlap (the width of the unpressed binding strip), trim away the excess end of the strip.

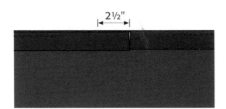

7. Open out both ends of the binding and align them as shown. Pin the ends together and draw a 45°-angle line from corner to corner.

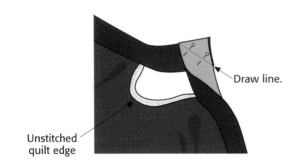

Draw line.

Unstitched quilt edge

8. Stitch on the line. Trim the seam to ¼" and then press it open. Use your fingers or a "wooden iron" to press. A wooden iron is a stick of wood with an angled end that you can use as a pressing tool.

Trim to ¼" and press open.

9. Refold the binding and stitch it to the quilt top, overlapping the beginning and ending stitches.

10. Trim the backing and batting even with the quilt-top edges if you have not already done so. Fold the binding over the quilt edge to the back and stitch it in place, mitering the corners.

LABELING YOUR QUILT

Congratulations! Now you have a finished quilt—well, almost. The last step is adding a label to document your work. The label doesn't have to be fancy, but it can be as elaborate as you wish to make it. For the simplest label, use a permanent fabric-marking pen to write pertinent information on a piece of plain muslin. Include your name, the name of the quilt pattern, and the date you finished the quilt. If the quilt is a gift, include the name of the recipient and the occasion for which it was made.

Some quilters like to keep a short documentation sheet, along with a photo of the quilt, in a personal quilt album. Include the same details you put on the label along with other significant information, such as notes about the fabric and any changes you may have made to the design. Perhaps you will want to include information about the fabric trade that provided the 5" squares for the quilt.

Shoo Fly

By Pat Speth, 71" x 101"

Finished block size: 10"

~ Skill Level: Beginner ~

This delightful quilt is easy to piece and perfect for a beginner. The quilt is made from two blocks—the positive and negative versions of the Shoo Fly block. I made this quilt with an assortment of large- and medium-scale floral prints. The value of the prints ranged from light to dark in relationship to each other but were all dark in relationship to the background fabric. You could choose medium and light values for a mellow look or try dark prints for a bolder, more dramatic effect.

QUILT SIZES AND STATISTICS

	Lap	Twin	Queen
Size	51" x 61"	71" x 101"	111" x 111"
Block A	10	27	50
Block B	10	27	50
Block set	4 x 5	6 x 9	10 x 10

MATERIALS

42"-wide fabric (40" of usable width after preshrinking and removing selvages)

	Lap	Twin	Queen
5" dark squares	30 pairs 3 singles	81 pairs 7 singles	150 pairs 13 singles
Background (light)	1⅜ yards	3⅜ yards	6 yards
Inner border	⅜ yard	½ yard	⅝ yard
Outer border and binding	1⅝ yards	2⅛ yards	2⅝ yards
Backing	3¼ yards	6 yards	9⅞ yards
Batting	55" x 65"	75" x 105"	115" x 115"

CUTTING

Cut all strips across the fabric width (crosswise grain).

Lap Size

	First Cut		Second Cut	
	Number of Strips	Strip Width	Number of Pieces	Piece Size
Background	5	5"	40	5" x 5"
	6	2½"	40	2½" x 4½"
			10	2½" x 2½"
Inner border	6	1½"		
Outer border	6	4¾"		
Binding	7	2½"		

Twin Size

	First Cut		Second Cut	
	Number of Strips	Strip Width	Number of Pieces	Piece Size
Background	14	5"	108	5" x 5"
	15	2½"	108	2½" x 4½"
			27	2½" x 2½"
Inner border	9	1½"		
Outer border	9	4¾"		
Binding	10	2½"		

Queen Size

	First Cut		Second Cut	
	Number of Strips	Strip Width	Number of Pieces	Piece Size
Background	25	5"	200	5" x 5"
	27	2½"	200	2½" x 4½"
			50	2½" x 2½"
Inner border	12	1½"		
Outer border	12	4¾"		
Binding	12	2½"		

MAKING THE BLOCKS

For each block A, you will use:

- 2 pairs of dark 5" squares
- 2 background 5" squares
- 1 background 2½" square

For each block B, you will use:

- 1 pair of dark 5" squares
- ¼ of a dark 5" square
- 2 background 5" squares
- 4 background 2½" x 4½" rectangles

1. Refer to "Half-Square-Triangle Units" on page 12 to make four half-square-triangle units for *each* block A and block B required, using one pair of dark squares and two background squares.

Make 4
for each block.

2. For *each* block A, trim away ½" from one side of a dark pair of squares. Cut the trimmed pieces in half in the opposite direction of the first cut, as shown, to yield four rectangles, 2½" x 4½".

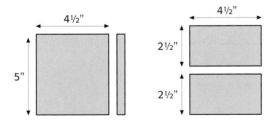

3. *To make each block A*, arrange four identical half-square-triangle units from step 1, four identical rectangles from step 2, and one background 2½" square into three horizontal rows as shown.

Sew the pieces in each row together; press the seams in the directions indicated. Sew the rows together; press the seams in the directions indicated.

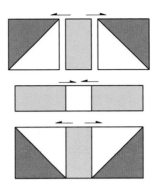
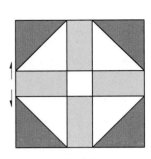

Block A

4. Cut the remaining dark squares in half lengthwise and crosswise. Each square will yield four 2½" squares.

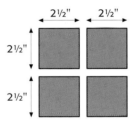

5. *To make each block B*, arrange four identical half-square-triangle units from step 1, four background 2½" x 4½" rectangles, and one dark 2½" square from step 4 into three horizontal rows as shown. Sew the pieces in each row together; press the seams in the directions indicated. Sew the rows together; press the seams in the directions indicated.

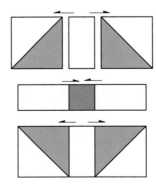
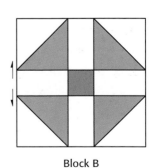

Block B

ASSEMBLING THE QUILT TOP

1. Refer to the quilt plan to arrange the blocks in horizontal rows on a design wall, alternating block A and block B in each row and from row to row. Sew the blocks in each row together; press the seams in opposite directions from row to row. Sew the rows together; press the seams in one direction.

2. Refer to "Plain Borders" on page 18 to add the inner and outer borders to the quilt top.

FINISHING

1. Layer the quilt top with batting and backing; hand or machine baste the layers together (see page 20).

2. Quilt as desired, bind the edges, add a label, and enjoy your finished quilt.

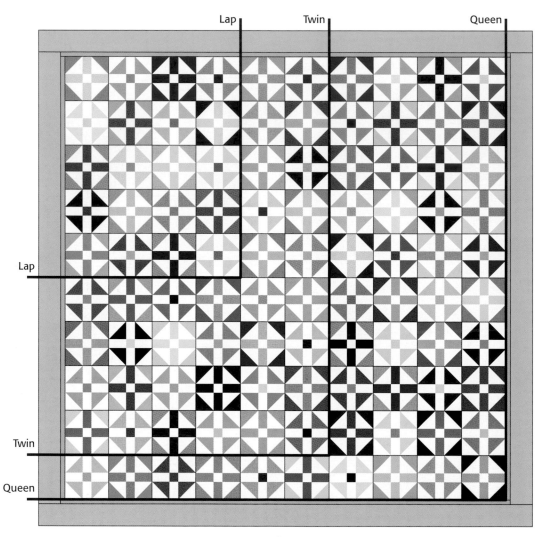

Quilt Plan

Streak of Lightning

By Pat Speth, 71" x 95"

Finished block size: 12"

~ Skill Level: Beginner ~

Assorted prints and plaids in mediums and darks are combined with various background fabrics to give this quilt a rustic look. Rotating every other block a quarter turn creates the design, but before you sew your blocks together, play with them on your design wall to see what other great arrangements you can create.

QUILT SIZES AND STATISTICS

	Lap	Twin	Queen
Size	59" x 59"	71" x 95"	107" x 107"
Number of blocks	16	35	64
Block set	4 x 4	5 x 7	8 x 8

MATERIALS

42"-wide fabric (40" of usable width after preshrinking and removing selvages)

	Lap	Twin	Queen
5" dark squares	76	167	304
5" light squares	68	149	272
Inner border	⅜ yard	½ yard	⅝ yard
Outer border and binding	1½ yards	2⅛ yards	2⅝ yards
Backing	3¾ yards	5¾ yards	9½ yards
Batting	63" x 63"	75" x 99"	111" x 111"

CUTTING

Cut all strips across the fabric width (crosswise grain).

Lap Size

	Number of Strips	Strip Width
Inner border	6	1½"
Outer border	6	4¾"
Binding	7	2½"

Twin Size

	Number of Strips	Strip Width
Inner border	9	1½"
Outer border	9	4¾"
Binding	9	2½"

Queen Size

	Number of Strips	Strip Width
Inner border	11	1½"
Outer border	11	4¾"
Binding	12	2½"

MAKING THE BLOCKS

For each block, you will use:

- 4¾ dark 5" squares
- 4¼ light 5" squares

1. Refer to "Two-Patch Units" on page 11 to sew dark and light squares together to make small two-patch units. Make nine small two-patch units for *each* block. Each set of one light and one dark square will yield four units. To determine the amount of sets required, multiply the number of

blocks required by nine and then divide by four. For instance, the lap-size quilt will require 36 sets: 16 blocks x 9 units in each block = 144 total units divided by 4 units per set = 36 sets.

Make 9
for each block.

2. Trim ½" from one side of each of the remaining dark and light squares. Cut each piece in half in the opposite direction of the first cut as shown. Each piece will yield two rectangles, 2½" x 4½".

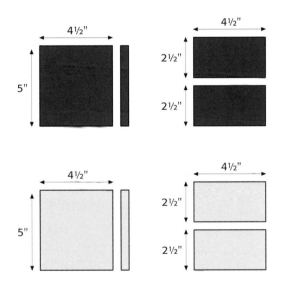

3. Stitch the dark and light rectangles to the two-patch units as shown, being careful to orient the two-patch units in the correct direction. Make five dark units and four light units for *each* block required.

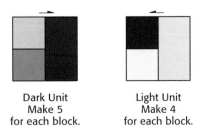

Dark Unit
Make 5
for each block.

Light Unit
Make 4
for each block.

4. *To make each block*, arrange the dark and light units into three horizontal rows as shown. Sew the units in each row together; press the seams in the directions indicated. Sew the rows together; press the seams in one direction.

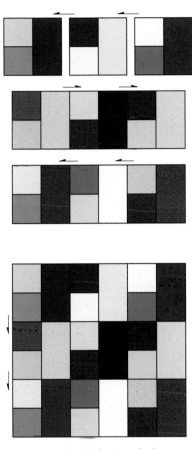

Streak of Lightning Block

ASSEMBLING THE QUILT TOP

1. Refer to the quilt plan to arrange the blocks in horizontal rows on your design wall, rotating every other block one-quarter turn to form the design. Sew the blocks in each row together; press the seams in opposite directions from row to row. Sew the rows together; press the seams in one direction.

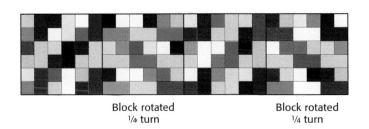

Block rotated
¼ turn

Block rotated
¼ turn

2. Refer to "Plain Borders" on page 18 to measure the quilt top to determine the cut length of the side inner and outer borders. Sew the inner-border strips to the outer-border strips and press the seams toward the outer border. Sew the combined side borders to the quilt top and press the seams toward the borders. Repeat to add the combined top and bottom borders to the quilt top.

FINISHING

1. Layer the quilt top with batting and backing; hand or machine baste the layers together (see page 20).

2. Quilt as desired, bind the edges, add a label, and enjoy your finished quilt.

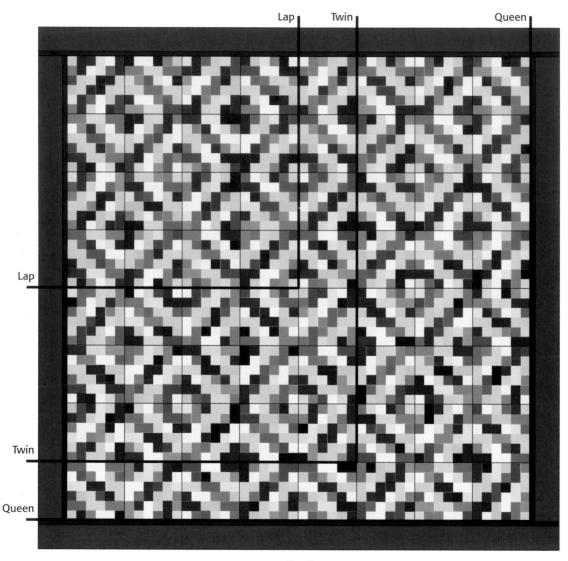

Quilt Plan

Beach Party

By Pat Speth, 75" x 99"

Finished block size: 8"

You might be tempted to put on sunglasses and sunblock while working on this quilt! The bright, bold fabrics will make a great quilt for any child. Florals, batiks, Christmas prints, and 1930s reproduction fabrics would also be good choices. Just be sure to use high-contrasting fabric colors or values in the half-square-triangle units for block A.

QUILT SIZES AND STATISTICS

	Lap	Twin	Queen
Size	51" x 51"	75" x 99"	107" x 107"
Block A	13	44	72
Block B	12	44	72
Block set	5 x 5	8 x 11	12 x 12

MATERIALS

42"-wide fabric (40" of usable width after preshrinking and removing selvages)

	Lap	Twin	Queen
5" bright squares	50	176	288
Background (light)	1⅛ yards	3⅜ yards	5½ yards
Inner border	⅜ yard	½ yard	⅝ yard
Outer border and binding	1½ yards	2⅛ yards	2⅝ yards
Backing	3¼ yards	6 yards	9½ yards
Batting	55" x 55"	79" x 103"	111" x 111"

CUTTING

Cut all strips across the fabric width (crosswise grain).

Lap Size

	First Cut		Second Cut	
	Number of Strips	Strip Width	Number of Pieces	Piece Size
Background	7	5"	50	5" x 5"
Inner border	6	1½"		
Outer border	6	4¾"		
Binding	6	2½"		

Twin Size

	First Cut		Second Cut	
	Number of Strips	Strip Width	Number of Pieces	Piece Size
Background	22	5"	176	5" x 5"
Inner border	9	1½"		
Outer border	9	4¾"		
Binding	10	2½"		

Queen Size

	First Cut		Second Cut	
	Number of Strips	Strip Width	Number of Pieces	Piece Size
Background	36	5"	288	5" x 5"
Inner border	10	1½"		
Outer border	11	4¾"		
Binding	12	2½"		

MAKING THE BLOCKS

For each block A and B, you will use:

- 2 different bright 5" squares
- 2 background 5" squares

1. For *each* block A, refer to "Half-Square-Triangle Units" on page 12 to sew bright and background squares together to make the units. Make two pairs of half-square-triangle units for *each* block A required. Press one pair of the units toward the background fabric and the other pair toward the bright fabric.

Make 2 pairs for each block A.

2. *To make each block A*, arrange the two pairs of half-square-triangle units from step 1 into two horizontal rows as shown. Sew the units in each row together; press the seam in the direction indicated. Sew the rows together; press the seam in the direction indicated.

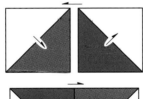
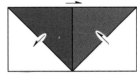
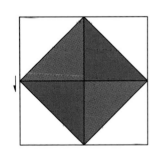

Block A

3. For *each* block B, refer to "Four-Patch Units" on page 11 to sew bright and background squares together to make four-patch units. Make two pairs of four-patch units for each block B required.

Make 2 pairs for each block B.

4. *To make each block B*, arrange two different pairs of units from step 3 into two horizontal rows as shown. Sew the units in each row together; press the seams in the directions indicated. Sew the rows together; press the seam in the direction indicated.

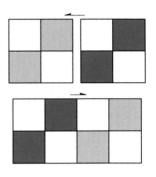 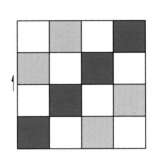

Block B

ASSEMBLING THE QUILT TOP

1. Refer to the quilt plan on page 34 to arrange the blocks in horizontal rows on your design wall, alternating block A and block B in each row and from row to row. Sew the blocks in each row together; press the seams in opposite directions from row to row. Sew the rows together; press the seams in one direction.

2. Refer to "Plain Borders" on page 18 to add the inner and outer borders to the quilt top.

FINISHING

1. Layer the quilt top with batting and backing; hand or machine baste the layers together (see page 20).

2. Quilt as desired, bind the edges, add a label, and enjoy your finished quilt.

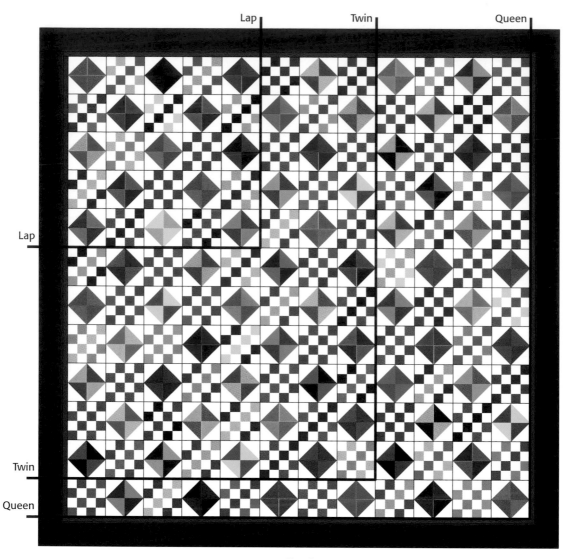

Quilt Plan

Jacob's Ladder

By Pat Speth, 72" x 108"

Finished block size: 12"

~ Skill Level: Beginner ~

What a difference a background can make! The same bright fabrics that were used in "Beach Party" on page 31 were used in this Jacob's Ladder quilt. The black background fabric makes the print fabrics glow. This easy-to-piece quilt will brighten up any room.

QUILT SIZES AND STATISTICS

	Lap	Twin	Queen
Size	60" x 60"	72" x 108"	108" x 108"
Number of blocks	16	40	64
Block set	4 x 4	5 x 8	8 x 8

MATERIALS

42"-wide fabric (40" of usable width after preshrinking and removing selvages)

	Lap	Twin	Queen
5" bright squares	72	180	288
Background (dark)	1½ yards	3⅝ yards	5½ yards
Inner border	½ yard	⅝ yard	¾ yard
Outer border and binding	1½ yards	2⅛ yards	2⅝ yards
Backing	3¾ yards	6⅜ yards	9½ yards
Batting	64" x 64"	76" x 112"	112" x 112"

CUTTING

Cut all strips across the fabric width (crosswise grain).

Lap Size

	First Cut		Second Cut	
	Number of Strips	Strip Width	Number of Pieces	Piece Size
Background	9	5"	72	5" x 5"
Inner border	6	2"		
Outer border	6	4¾"		
Binding	7	2½"		

Twin Size

	First Cut		Second Cut	
	Number of Strips	Strip Width	Number of Pieces	Piece Size
Background	23	5"	180	5" x 5"
Inner border	9	2"		
Outer border	9	4¾"		
Binding	10	2½"		

Queen Size

	First Cut		Second Cut	
	Number of Strips	Strip Width	Number of Pieces	Piece Size
Background	36	5"	288	5" x 5"
Inner border	10	2"		
Outer border	11	4¾"		
Binding	12	2½"		

MAKING THE BLOCKS

For each block, you will use:

- 4½ bright 5" squares
- 4½ background 5" squares

1. Refer to "Half-Square-Triangle Units" on page 12 to sew bright and background squares together to make half-square-triangle units. Make four units for *each* block required.

Make 4
for each block.

2. Refer to "Four-Patch Units" on page 11 to use the remaining bright and dark squares to make scrappy four-patch units. Make five scrappy four-patch units for each block required.

Make 5
for each block.

3. *To make each block*, arrange four half-square-triangle units and five four-patch units into horizontal rows as shown. Sew the units in each row together; press the seams in the directions indicated. Sew the rows together; press the seams in the directions indicated.

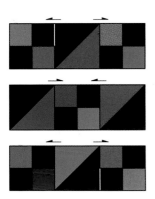

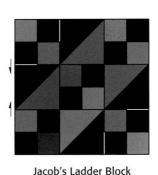

Jacob's Ladder Block

ASSEMBLING THE QUILT TOP

1. Refer to the quilt plan on page 38 to arrange the blocks in horizontal rows on your design wall, rotating every other block one-quarter turn to form the design. Sew the blocks in each row together; press the seams in opposite directions from row to row. Sew the rows together; press the seams in one direction.

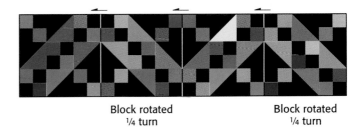

Block rotated
¼ turn

Block rotated
¼ turn

2. Refer to "Plain Borders" on page 18 to add the inner and outer borders to the quilt top.

FINISHING

1. Layer the quilt top with batting and backing; hand or machine baste the layers together (see page 20).
2. Quilt as desired, bind the edges, add a label, and enjoy your finished quilt.

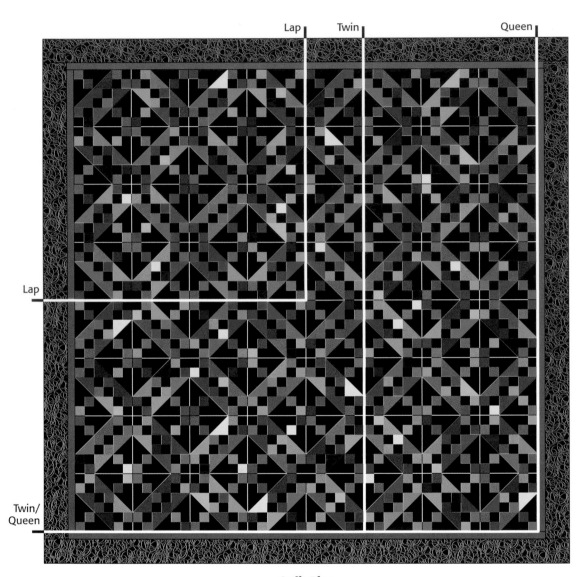

Quilt Plan

Idaho Beauty

By Pat Speth, 75" x 107"

Finished block size: 32"

∽ *Skill Level: Beginner* ∽

This big-block quilt is easy to piece with four-patch and half-square-triangle units. Dark and medium prints are teamed with plaids to create the rustic look. The inner- and outer-border strips are pieced before applying them to the quilt top to make construction even easier.

QUILT SIZES AND STATISTICS

	Lap	Twin	Queen
Size	75" x 75"	75" x 107"	107" x 107"
Number of blocks	4	6	9
Block set	2 x 2	2 x 3	3 x 3

MATERIALS

42"-wide fabric (40" of usable width after preshrinking and removing selvages)

	Lap	Twin	Queen
5" dark squares	96	144	216
4½" dark squares*	16	24	36
5" light squares	96	144	216
4½" light squares*	48	72	108
Inner border	½ yard	½ yard	⅝ yard
Outer border and binding	2 yards	2⅛ yards	2⅝ yards
Backing	4⅝ yards	6⅜ yards	9½ yards
Batting	79" x 79"	79" x 111"	111" x 111"

* If you already have an assortment of 5" squares, simply trim the squares to 4½" x 4½".

CUTTING

Cut all strips across the fabric width (crosswise grain).

Lap Size

	Number of Strips	Strip Width
Inner border	8	1½"
Outer border	8	4¾"
Binding	9	2½"

Twin Size

	Number of Strips	Strip Width
Inner border	9	1½"
Outer border	9	4¾"
Binding	10	2½"

Queen Size

	Number of Strips	Strip Width
Inner border	11	1½"
Outer border	11	4¾"
Binding	12	2½"

MAKING THE BLOCKS

For each block, you will use:

- 24 dark 5" squares
- 4 dark 4½" squares
- 24 light 5" squares
- 12 light 4½" squares

1. Refer to "Four-Patch Units" on page 11 to sew dark and light 5" squares together to make scrappy four-patch units. Make 16 for *each* block required.

Make 16
for each block.

2. Refer to "Half-Square-Triangle Units" on page 12 to sew dark and light 5" squares together to make half-square-triangle units. Make 32 for *each* block required. Press half of the units' seams toward the dark fabric and the other half toward the light fabric before trimming the units to 4½".

Make 16
for each block.

Make 16
for each block.

3. Arrange four four-patch units, eight half-square-triangle units, three light 4½" squares, and one dark 4½" square into horizontal rows as shown, paying careful attention to the placement of the half-square-triangle units. Stitch the pieces in each row together; press the seams in the directions indicated. Sew the rows together; press the seams in the directions indicated. Make four units for each block.

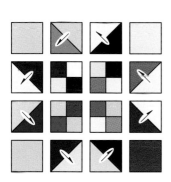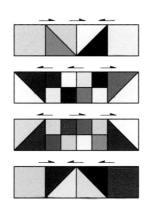

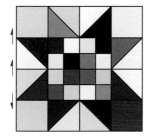

Make 4
for each block.

4. *To make each block,* arrange four units from step 3 into two horizontal rows, placing the dark square in each unit so that it will be in the center of the finished block. Sew the units in each row together; press the seams in opposite directions. Sew the rows together; press the seams in one direction.

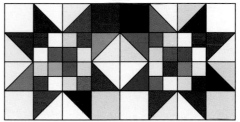

Idaho Beauty Block

ASSEMBLING THE QUILT TOP

1. Refer to the quilt plan to arrange the blocks in horizontal rows on your design wall. Sew the blocks in each row together; press the seams in opposite directions from row to row. Sew the rows together; press the seams in one direction.

2. Refer to "Plain Borders" on page 18 to measure the quilt top to determine the cut length of the side inner and outer borders. Sew the inner-border strips to the outer-border strips and press the seams toward the outer border. Sew the combined side borders to the quilt top and press the seam toward the borders. Repeat to add the combined top and bottom borders to the quilt top.

FINISHING

1. Layer the quilt top with batting and backing; hand or machine baste the layers together (see page 20).

2. Quilt as desired, bind the edges, add a label, and enjoy your finished quilt.

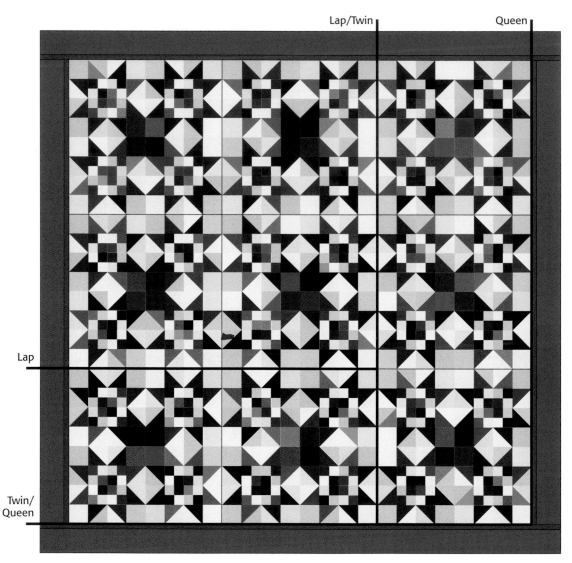

Quilt Plan

Path and Stiles

By Pat Speth, 74" x 102"

Finished block size: 14"

~ *Skill Level: Easy* ~

The longtime favorite traditional Path and Stiles block makes great use of assorted prints, plaids, and background squares. The easy-to-piece striped border adds the finishing touch. Consider other fabric choices, such as batiks or 1800s reproduction prints, or pair bright and bold fabrics with a black background.

QUILT SIZES AND STATISTICS

	Lap	Twin	Queen
Size	60" x 60"	74" x 102"	102" x 102"
Number of blocks	9	24	36
Block set	3 x 3	4 x 6	6 x 6

MATERIALS

42"-wide fabric (40" of usable width after preshrinking and removing selvages)

	Lap	Twin	Queen
5" dark squares	73	165	235
5" light squares	88	207	298
Borders and binding	1⅝ yards	2⅜ yards	2⅝ yards
Backing	3¾ yards	6⅛ yards	9 yards
Batting	64" x 64"	78" x 106"	106" x 106"

CUTTING

Cut all strips across the fabric width (crosswise grain).

NOTE: Wait to cut the strips for the inner border until the quilt top is finished (refer to "Pieced Borders" on page 19).

Lap Size

	Number of Strips	Strip Width
Inner border	5	2½"
Outer border	6	3¼"
Binding	7	2½"

Twin Size

	Number of Strips	Strip Width
Inner border	9	2½"
Outer border	9	3¼"
Binding	10	2½"

Queen Size

	Number of Strips	Strip Width
Inner border	10	2½"
Outer border	11	3¼"
Binding	11	2½"

MAKING THE BLOCKS

For each block, you will use:

- 7 light 5" squares
- 5¼ dark 5" squares

1. Refer to "Half-Square-Triangle Units" on page 12 to sew light and dark squares together to make half-square-triangle units. Make four for *each* block required.

Make 4
for each block.

2. Refer to "Two-Patch Units" on page 11 to sew light and dark squares together to make large two-patch units. Make four units for *each* block required.

Make 4
for each block.

3. For *each* block, trim away ½" from one side of two light 5" squares. Cut the trimmed pieces in half in the opposite direction of the first cut, as shown, to yield four rectangles, 2½" x 4½".

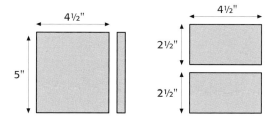

4. Sew one rectangle from step 3 to each large two-patch unit from step 2 as shown. Press the seams toward the dark rectangles.

 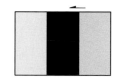

5. Refer to "Four-Patch Units" on page 11 to sew dark and light squares together to make four-patch units. Make one unit for *each* block required.

Make 1
for each block.

6. Refer to "Two-Patch Units" on page 11 to sew dark and light squares together to make small two-patch units. Make two units for *each* block required.

Make 2
for each block.

7. Divide the number of blocks required for the quilt size you are making by 4 and round up to the nearest whole number. Cut that amount of dark 5" squares in half lengthwise and crosswise. Each square will yield four 2½" squares.

8. Sew one four-patch unit, two small two-patch units, and one dark 2½" square together as shown.

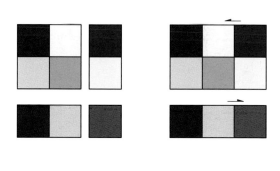

9. *To make each block,* arrange four half-square-triangle units, four units from step 4, and one unit from step 8 into horizontal rows as shown. Sew the pieces in each row together; press the seams in the directions indicated. Sew the rows together; press the seams in the directions indicated.

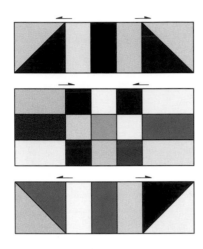

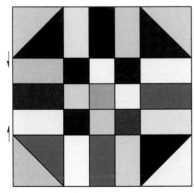

Path and Stiles Block

MAKING THE PIECED BORDER

Pieced-Border Units

	Lap	Twin	Queen
Side border units	11½ per strip	22 per strip	22 per strip
Top and bottom border units	13½ per strip	17 per strip	24 per strip
Total border units	50	78	92

1. Refer to "Two-Patch Units" on page 11 to sew dark and light squares together to make the required number of large two-patch units for the quilt size you are making. Each border unit is equal to one large two-patch unit. *For the lap-size quilt,* make only the number of whole units required. The half units will be added later.

Make 1 for each border unit required.

2. Sew the required number of large two-patch units together to complete each border strip. Press the seams in one direction. *For the lap-size quilt only,* trim away ½" from one side of two dark 5" squares. Cut the trimmed pieces in half in the opposite direction of the first cut to yield four rectangles, 2½" x 4½". Stitch one rectangle to one end of each border strip.

For lap size only: Add a 2½" x 4½" piece to complete the border strip.

ASSEMBLING THE QUILT TOP

1. Refer to the quilt plan to arrange the blocks in horizontal rows on your design wall. Sew the blocks in each row together; press the seams in opposite directions from row to row. Sew the rows together; press the seams in one direction.

2. Refer to "Pieced Borders" on page 19 to add the inner, pieced, and outer borders to the quilt top.

FINISHING

1. Layer the quilt top with batting and backing; hand or machine baste the layers together (see page 20).

2. Quilt as desired, bind the edges, add a label, and enjoy your finished quilt.

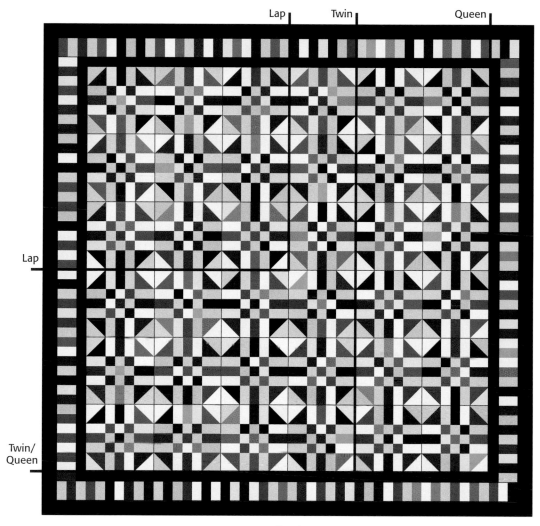

Quilt Plan

Pinwheels on Parade

By Pat Speth and Roxie Speth, 51" x 51"

Finished block size: 8"

Skill Level: Easy

A picket-fence unit is used in each section of the block to create the pinwheel. My daughter, Roxie, and I used a large assortment of batik and background fabrics in this quilt, but 1930s reproduction prints, brights, and rustic-looking fabrics would also be good choices.

QUILT SIZES AND STATISTICS

	Lap	Twin	Queen
Size	51" x 51"	75" x 99"	107" x 107"
Block A	13	44	72
Block B	12	44	72
Block set	5 x 5	8 x 11	12 x 12

MATERIALS

42"-wide fabric (40" of usable width after preshrinking and removing selvages)

	Lap	Twin	Queen
5" dark squares	64	220	360
5" light squares	61	220	360
Inner border	⅜ yard	½ yard	⅝ yard
Outer border and binding	1¼ yards	2⅛ yards	2⅝ yards
Backing	3¼ yards	5⅞ yards	9½ yards
Batting	55" x 55"	79" x 103"	111" x 111"

CUTTING

Cut all strips across the fabric width (crosswise grain).

Lap Size

	Number of Strips	Strip Width
Inner border	5	1½"
Outer border	5	4¾"
Binding	6	2½"

Twin Size

	Number of Strips	Strip Width
Inner border	9	1½"
Outer border	9	4¾"
Binding	10	2½"

Queen Size

	Number of Strips	Strip Width
Inner border	10	1½"
Outer border	11	4¾"
Binding	12	2½"

MAKING THE BLOCKS

For each block A, you will use:

- 1 light 5" square
- 4 dark 5" squares

For each block B, you will use:

- 4 light 5" squares
- 1 dark 5" square

1. For *each* block A, cut a light 5" square in half lengthwise and crosswise. Each square will yield four 2½" squares.

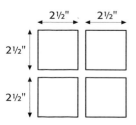

2. Refer to "Picket-Fence Units" on page 15 to trim and cut one dark 5" square into two rectangles, 2½" x 4½". Using one light 2½" square from step 1 and one rectangle, make one picket-fence unit. Pay careful attention to the placement of the light triangle on the unit. Sew the picket-fence unit to the remaining rectangle. Repeat to make four units for each block A. Press the seams toward the solid rectangles.

Make 4
for each block A.

3. *To make each block A,* arrange four units from step 2 into two horizontal rows as shown. Sew the units in each row together; press the seams in opposite directions. Sew the rows together; press the seams in one direction.

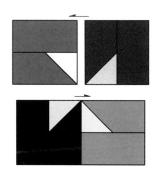 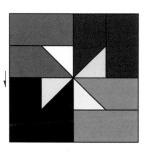

Block A

4. For *each* block B, cut one dark 5" square in half lengthwise and crosswise to yield four 2½" squares.

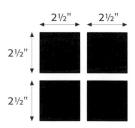

5. Refer to "Picket-Fence Units" on page 15 to trim and cut one light 5" square into two rectangles, 2½" x 4½". Using one dark 2½" square from step 4 and one rectangle, make one picket-fence unit. Pay careful attention to the placement of the dark triangle on the unit. Sew the picket-fence unit to the remaining rectangle. Repeat to make four units for each block B. Press the seams toward the solid rectangles.

Make 4
for each block B.

6. *To make each block B,* arrange four units from step 5 into two horizontal rows as shown. Sew the units in each row together; press the seams in opposite directions. Sew the rows together; press the seams in one direction.

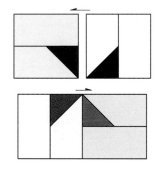 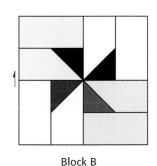

Block B

ASSEMBLING THE QUILT TOP

1. Refer to the quilt plan on page 51 to arrange the blocks in horizontal rows on your design wall, alternating block A and block B in each row and from row to row. Sew the blocks in each row together; press the seams in opposite directions from row to row. Sew the rows together; press the seams in one direction.

2. Refer to "Plain Borders" on page 18 to add the inner and outer borders to the quilt top.

FINISHING

1. Layer the quilt top with batting and backing; hand or machine baste the layers together (see page 20).

2. Quilt as desired, bind the edges, add a label, and enjoy your finished quilt.

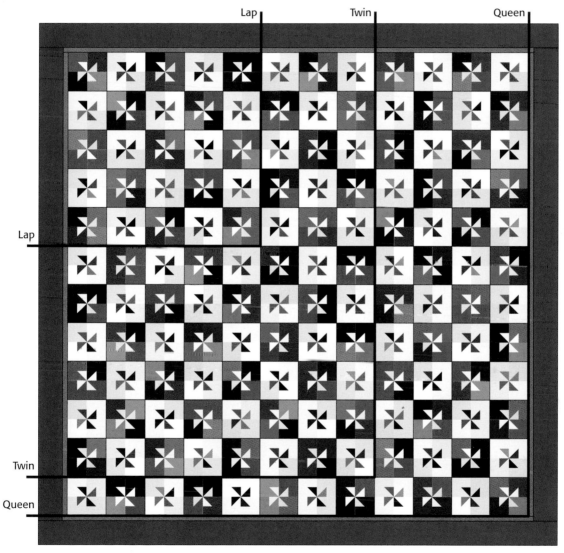

Quilt Plan

Star and Hourglass

By Pat Speth, 67" x 98½"

Finished block size: 7"

~ Skill Level: Easy ~

Because the hourglass and small-wonders units finish to the same size, they were a natural choice to bring together in a quilt. I used a large variety of reds, blues, and creams to create this easy quilt, which can be used and enjoyed throughout the year. For a change of pace, use reds for the star units and greens for the hourglass units and you'll be set for Christmas. Or, go completely scrappy and don't worry about color placement.

QUILT SIZES AND STATISTICS

	Lap	Twin	Queen
Size	56½" x 56½"	67" x 98½"	109" x 109"
Number of blocks	16	40	81
Block set	4 x 4	5 x 8	9 x 9
Sashing blocks	40	93	180

MATERIALS

42"-wide fabric (40" of usable width after preshrinking and removing selvages)

	Lap	Twin	Queen
5" blue squares	32	80	162
5" red squares	40	93	180
5" light squares	72	173	342
4" light squares*	25	54	100
Inner border	⅜ yard	½ yard	⅝ yard
Outer borders and binding	1½ yards	2⅛ yards	2⅝ yards
Backing	3⅝ yards	5⅞ yards	9⅝ yards
Batting	61" x 61"	71" x 103"	113" x 113"

* If you already have an assortment of 5" light squares, simply trim the squares to 4" x 4".

CUTTING

Cut all strips across the fabric width (crosswise grain).

Lap Size

	Number of Strips	Strip Width
Inner border	6	1½"
Outer border	6	4¾"
Binding	7	2½"

Twin Size

	Number of Strips	Strip Width
Inner border	8	1½"
Outer border	9	4¾"
Binding	9	2½"

Queen Size

	Number of Strips	Strip Width
Inner border	11	1½"
Outer border	12	4¾"
Binding	12	2½"

MAKING THE BLOCKS

For each Star block, you will use:

- 2 blue 5" squares
- 2 light 5" squares

For each sashing block, you will use:

- 1 red 5" square
- 1 light 5" square

1. Refer to "Small-Wonders Units" on page 13 to sew the blue and light 5" squares together to make half-square-triangle units. Make four for *each* block required. Press half the units' seams toward the dark fabric and the other half toward the light

fabric. Cut the half-square-triangle units into small-wonders units.

Half-Square-Triangle Units
Make 4 for each block.

Small-Wonders Units

2. Arrange the small-wonders units from each half-square-triangle unit into two horizontal rows as shown, paying careful attention to the orientation of each half-square-triangle unit. Sew the units in each row together; press the seams in the directions indicated. Sew the rows together; press the seam in the direction indicated.

3. *To make each Star block,* arrange four different units from step 2 into two horizontal rows as shown. Sew the units in each row together; press the seams in the directions indicated. Sew the rows together; press the seam in the direction indicated.

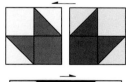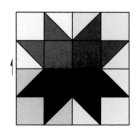

Star Block

4. Refer to "Hourglass Units" on page 14 to sew the red and light 5" squares together to make hourglass units. Make two for *each* sashing block required. Sew the hourglass units together in pairs; press the seam in the direction indicated.

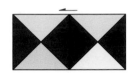

Sashing Block

ASSEMBLING THE QUILT TOP

1. Refer to the quilt plan to alternately sew the 4" light squares and the sashing blocks together as shown to form the sashing rows, beginning and ending with a light square. Press the seams toward the squares. Make the number of horizontal sashing rows required. Alternately sew the Star blocks and the remaining sashing blocks together to form the block rows, beginning and ending with a sashing block. Press the seams toward the Star blocks. Make the number of block rows required.

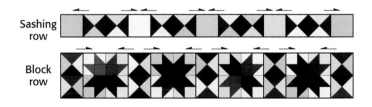

Sashing row

Block row

2. Alternately sew the block rows and the sashing rows together to complete the quilt top, beginning and ending with a sashing row. Press the seams in one direction.

3. Refer to "Plain Borders" on page 18 to add the inner and outer borders to the quilt top.

FINISHING

1. Layer the quilt top with batting and backing; hand or machine baste the layers together (see page 20).

2. Quilt as desired, bind the edges, add a label, and enjoy your finished quilt.

Lap   Twin   Queen

Lap

Twin

Queen

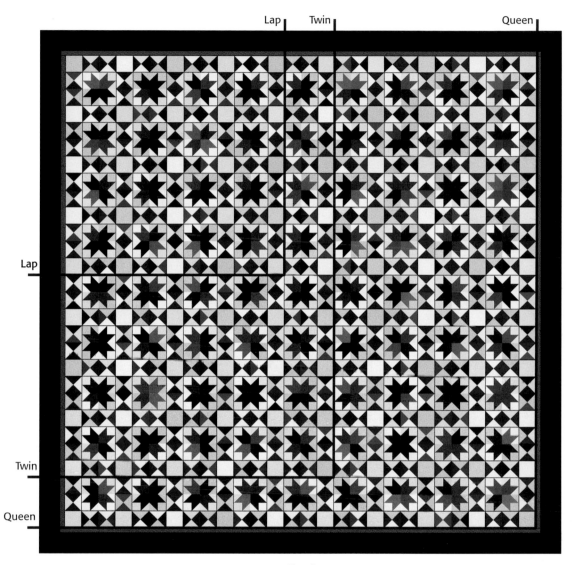

Quilt Plan

King's Crown

By Pat Speth, 67½" x 95½"

Finished block size: 8"

~ Skill Level: Easy ~

For this quilt, dig into your stash of 1800s prints and start seeing what fun fabric combinations you can come up with. I used squares of the same dark fabric to make the small squares in one block and different light fabrics for the sashing squares. For some of the flying-geese units, I used two prints that were very close in color for each block; for others, I used high-contrasting fabrics.

QUILT SIZES AND STATISTICS

	Lap	Twin	Queen
Size	53⅜" x 67½"	67½" x 95¾"	109¾" x 109¾"
Number of blocks	18	39	85
Diagonal block set	3 x 4	4 x 6	7 x 7

MATERIALS

42"-wide fabric (40" of usable width after preshrinking and removing selvages)

	Lap	Twin	Queen
5" dark squares	102	213	451
5" light squares	44	93	198
4½" light squares*	18	39	85
Setting triangles	¾ yard	⅞ yard	1⅛ yards
Inner border	⅜ yard	½ yard	⅝ yard
Outer border and binding	1½ yards	2 yards	2⅝ yards
Backing	3⅜ yards	5¾ yards	9⅝ yards
Batting	58" x 72"	72" x 100"	114" x 114"

* If you already have an assortment of 5" light squares, simply trim the squares to 4½" x 4½".

CUTTING

Cut all strips across the fabric width (crosswise grain).

Lap Size

	First Cut		Second Cut	
	Number of Strips	Strip Width	Number of Pieces	Piece Size
Setting triangles	1	12⅝"	3	12⅝" x 12⅝"
	1	6⅝"	2	6⅝" x 6⅝"
Inner border	6	1½"		
Outer border	6	4¾"		
Binding	7	2½"		

Twin Size

	First Cut		Second Cut	
	Number of Strips	Strip Width	Number of Pieces	Piece Size
Setting triangles	2	12⅝"	4	12⅝" x 12⅝"
			2	6⅝" x 6⅝"
Inner border	8	1½"		
Outer border	8	4¾"		
Binding	9	2½"		

Queen Size

	First Cut		Second Cut	
	Number of Strips	Strip Width	Number of Pieces	Piece Size
Setting triangles	2	12⅝"	6	12⅝" x 12⅝"
	1	6⅝"	2	6⅝" x 6⅝"
Inner border	11	1½"		
Outer border	11	4¾"		
Binding	12	2½"		

MAKING THE BLOCKS

For each block, you will use:

- 2 light 5" squares
- 3 dark 5" squares
- 1 light 4½" square

1. Cut all of the light 5" squares in half lengthwise and crosswise. For *each* block required, cut one dark 5" square in half lengthwise and crosswise. Each square will yield four 2½" squares.

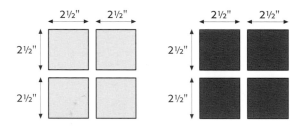

2. Refer to "Flying-Geese Units" on page 17 to use the light 2½" squares from step 1 and the dark 5" squares to make flying-geese units. Make four flying-geese units for *each* block.

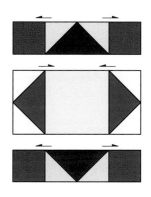

Make 4
for each block.

3. *To make each block,* arrange four flying-geese units, four dark 2½" squares, and one light 4½" square into three horizontal rows as shown. Sew the pieces in each row together; press the seams away from the flying-geese units. Sew the rows together; press the seams in the directions indicated.

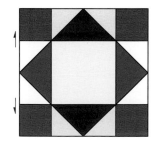

King's Crown Block

ASSEMBLING THE QUILT TOP

1. Cut the remaining dark 5" squares in half as shown and sew the two resulting rectangles from each square together end to end. Trim ½" from each end so that the sashing piece measures 2½" x 8½".

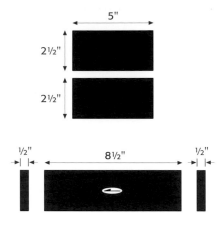

2. Cut the 6⅝" setting triangle squares in half once diagonally to yield four corner triangles.

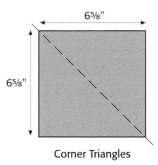

Corner Triangles

3. Cut the 12⅝" setting triangle squares in half twice diagonally. Each square will yield four side setting triangles.

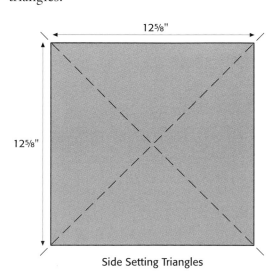

Side Setting Triangles

4. Referring to the quilt plan on page 60 for the size you are making, arrange the blocks, setting triangles, sashing strips, and 2½" light squares in diagonal rows on your design wall. Sew the pieces in each row together; press the seams toward the sashing strips. The outer 2½" squares in each sashing row will extend beyond the setting triangles. Stitch the rows together; press the seams in one direction. Add the corner triangles last.

NOTE: The lap-size quilt plan is shown here.

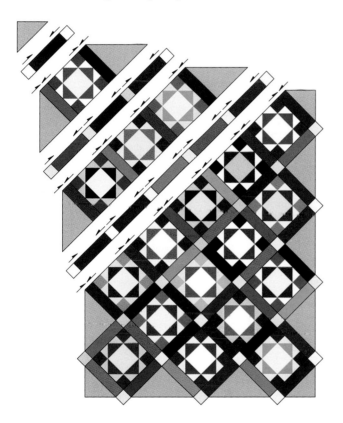

5. Using a ruler and rotary cutter, trim the excess from the setting triangles, leaving a ¼"-wide seam allowance beyond the outer points of the sashing strips.

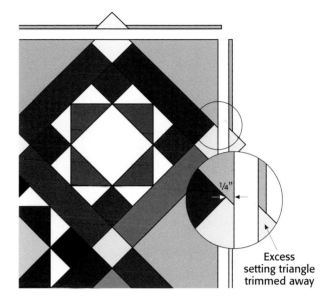

1/4"

Excess
setting triangle
trimmed away

6. Refer to "Plain Borders" on page 18 to add the inner and outer borders to the quilt top.

FINISHING

1. Layer the quilt top with batting and backing; hand or machine baste the layers together (see page 20).

2. Quilt as desired, bind the edges, add a label, and enjoy your finished quilt.

Lap-Size Quilt Plan

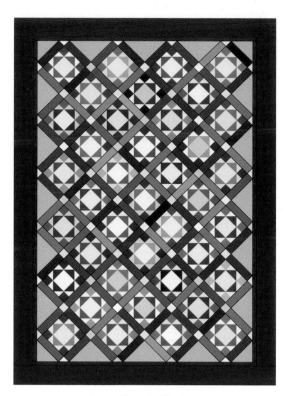

Twin-Size Quilt Plan

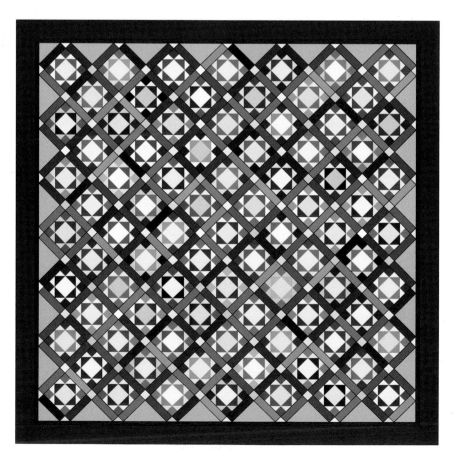

Queen-Size Quilt Plan

Woodland Clover

By Pat Speth, 66" x 98"

Finished block size: 8"

〜 *Skill Level: Easy* 〜

This quilt is a delight to make! One simple unit makes the Woodland Clover block and the Picket Fence border block; all you do is change the placement of light and dark fabrics in the unit. I chose a variety of prints and plaids, but this quilt would also look great in batiks, 1930s reproduction prints, Christmas prints, or florals.

QUILT SIZES AND STATISTICS

	Lap	Twin	Queen
Size	58" x 58"	66" x 98"	106" x 106"
Number of blocks	16	40	81
Block set	4 x 4	5 x 8	9 x 9

MATERIALS

42"-wide fabric (40" of usable width after preshrinking and removing selvages)

	Lap	Twin	Queen
5" print squares	52	111	206
5" plaid squares	52	111	206
5" light squares	92	201	378
Borders and binding	1¾ yards	2⅜ yards	3 yards
Backing	3⅝ yards	5⅞ yards	9⅜ yards
Batting	62" x 62"	70" x 102"	110" x 110"

CUTTING

Cut all strips across the fabric width (crosswise grain).

NOTE: Wait to cut the strips for the inner border until the quilt top is finished (refer to "Pieced Borders" on page 19).

Lap Size

	Number of Strips	Strip Width
Inner border	5	3½"
Outer border	6	3¼"
Binding	7	2½"

Twin Size

	Number of Strips	Strip Width
Inner border (sides)	4	2½"
Inner border (top/bottom)	3	3½"
Outer border	9	3¼"
Binding	9	2½"

Queen Size

	Number of Strips	Strip Width
Inner border	10	2½"
Outer border	12	3¼"
Binding	12	2½"

MAKING THE BLOCKS

For each block, you will use:

- 2 light 5" squares
- 2 print 5" squares
- 2 plaid 5" squares

1. For *each* block, cut two light squares in half lengthwise and crosswise. Each square will yield four 2½" squares.

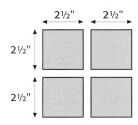

2. For *each* block, refer to "Picket-Fence Units" on page 15 to trim and cut two print and two plaid squares into rectangles. Each square will yield two rectangles, 2½" x 4½". Use these rectangles and the light 2½" squares from step 1 to make the picket-fence units. Press the plaid units' seams in the opposite direction as the print units' seams. Stitch one print unit and one plaid unit together as shown. Press the seams toward the plaid units.

**Make 4
for each block.**

3. *To make each block,* arrange the picket-fence units into two horizontal rows of two units each as shown. Stitch the units in each row together; press the seams in opposite directions. Sew the rows together; press the seam in the direction indicated.

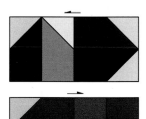 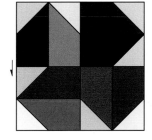

MAKING THE SASHING PIECES

	Lap	Twin	Queen
Sashing strips	24	67	144
Sashing squares	9	28	64

1. Cut one light 5" square in half as shown for *each* sashing strip required. Sew the rectangles together in pairs as shown, using rectangles cut from different fabrics. Trim ½" from each end so that the sashing strip measures 2½" x 8½".

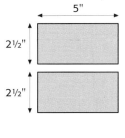

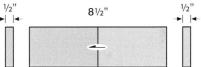

2. Divide the number of sashing squares required by four and round up to the nearest whole number. Cut that number of 5" dark (plaid or print) squares in half lengthwise and crosswise. Each square will yield four 2½" squares.

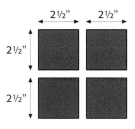

To add more variety to the sashing squares in the twin-size quilt, cut nine plaid and/or print squares in half lengthwise. Cut one of the resulting rectangles from each square in half crosswise to yield two 2½" squares. Use one square for the sashing. Trim ½" from one end of the rectangles so that they measure 2½" x 4½". Use the trimmed rectangles and the remaining square for the border picket-fence units.

MAKING THE PIECED BORDER

Pieced-Border Units

	Lap	Twin	Queen
Left side border units	11	21	23
Right side border units	12	22	24
Top border units	12	14	24
Bottom border units	13	15	25
Total border units	48	72	96

1. Divide the total number of border units required by four and cut that number of 5" light and dark (print or plaid) squares in half lengthwise and crosswise. Each square will yield four 2½" squares. Refer to "Picket-Fence Units" on page 15 to trim and cut the remaining 5" light and dark squares into two rectangles *each*, 2½" x 4½". Using the light squares on the dark rectangles and vice versa, make the picket-fence units. Press the seams in the directions indicated.

Dark Picket-Fence Unit   Light Picket-Fence Unit

2. Sew each dark picket-fence unit to a light picket-fence unit as shown to form a border unit. Press the seam in the direction indicated.

3. Refer to the quilt plan to assemble the border strips. The borders will be added clockwise to the quilt, beginning with the left side. Note the orientation of the bottom left unit.

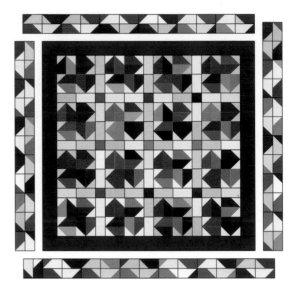

ASSEMBLING THE QUILT TOP

1. Referring to the quilt plan on page 65, alternately sew the blocks and sashing strips into horizontal rows as shown to form the block rows, beginning and ending with a block. Alternately sew the sashing strips and sashing squares into horizontal rows to form the sashing rows, beginning and ending with a sashing strip. Press the seams toward the sashing strips.

2. Alternately sew the block rows and sashing rows together to complete the quilt top, beginning and ending with a block row. Press the seams in one direction.

3. Refer to "Pieced Borders" on page 19 to add the inner borders to the quilt top. Stitch the pieced borders to the quilt top, beginning with the left side border and working clockwise. Stitch the outer border to the quilt top in the same manner as the inner border.

FINISHING

1. Layer the quilt top with batting and backing; hand or machine baste the layers together (see page 20).

2. Quilt as desired, bind the edges, add a label, and enjoy your finished quilt.

Lap   Twin   Queen

Lap

Twin

Queen

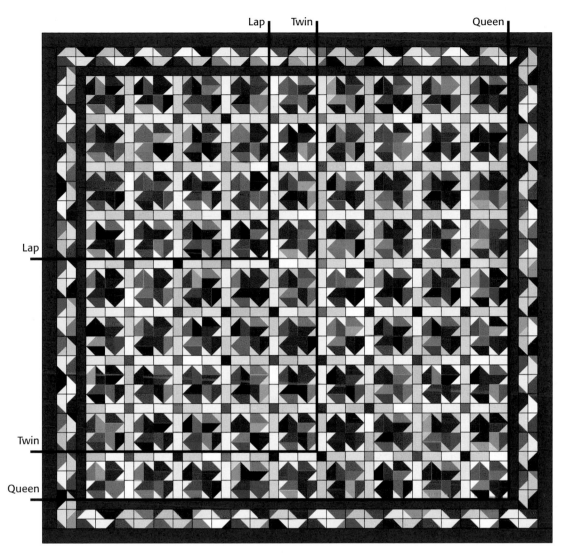

Quilt Plan

Stars over Mitford

By Pat Speth, 71" x 95"

Finished block size: 12"

∾ *Skill Level: Easy* ∾

Just like the stars in the sky, the stars in this quilt are there—you just don't always see them. Made with 1800s reproduction fabrics, this quilt is a great exercise tool for working with the placement of dark- and medium-value fabrics in a block. I've given several examples for the alternate placement of dark- and medium-value fabrics; use these, or create your own and have fun playing with your fabrics!

QUILT SIZES AND STATISTICS

	Lap	Twin	Queen
Size	59" x 59"	71" x 95"	107" x 107"
Number of blocks	16	35	64
Block set	4 x 4	5 x 7	8 x 8

MATERIALS

42"-wide fabric (40" of usable width after preshrinking and removing selvages)

	Lap	Twin	Queen
5" dark and/or medium squares	48 pairs 16 singles	105 pairs 35 singles	192 pairs 64 singles
5" light squares	32 pairs 16 singles	70 pairs 35 singles	128 pairs 64 singles
Inner border	⅜ yard	½ yard	⅝ yard
Outer border and binding	1½ yards	2⅛ yards	2⅝ yards
Backing	3¾ yards	5¾ yards	9½ yards
Batting	63" x 63"	75" x 99"	111" x 111"

CUTTING

Cut all strips across the fabric width (crosswise grain).

Lap Size

	Number of Strips	Strip Width
Inner border	6	1½"
Outer border	6	4¾"
Binding	7	2½"

Twin Size

	Number of Strips	Strip Width
Inner border	8	1½"
Outer border	9	4¾"
Binding	9	2½"

Queen Size

	Number of Strips	Strip Width
Inner border	10	1½"
Outer border	11	4¾"
Binding	12	2½"

MAKING THE BLOCKS

For each block, you will use:

- 3 different pairs of dark or medium 5" squares
- 1 dark or medium 5" square
- 2 different pairs of light 5" squares
- 1 light 5" square

1. Using one pair of dark or medium 5" squares and one pair of light squares, refer to "Half Square-Triangle Units" on page 12 to make four half-square-triangle units. Press the seams toward the light fabric.

Make 4.

2. Refer to "Flying-Geese Units" on page 17 to cut one pair of dark or medium 5" squares into 2½" squares and one pair of light 5" squares into 2½" x 4½" rectangles to make four flying-geese units.

Make 4.

3. Trim ½" from one edge of one pair of dark or medium 5" squares. Cut the trimmed pieces in half in the opposite direction of the first cut to yield four rectangles, 2½" x 4½".

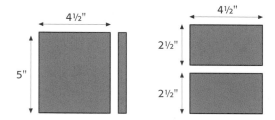

4. Sew a rectangle from step 3 to each flying-geese unit from step 2 as shown. Press the seams toward the rectangles.

5. Trim a dark or medium 5" square to 4½" x 4½". Cut a light 5" square in half lengthwise and cross-wise to yield four 2½" squares. Draw a diagonal line on the wrong side of the 2½" squares.

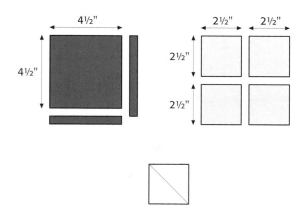

6. With right sides together, refer to "Sew and Flip" on page 16 to sew the 2½" light squares to each corner of the 4" square, stitching opposite corners first. Trim and press each 2½" square as shown.

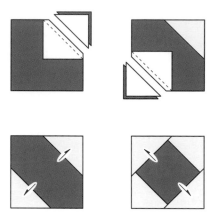

7. Arrange the four half-square-triangle units from step 1, the four flying-geese units from step 4, and the unit from step 6 into three horizontal rows as shown. Sew the units in each row together; press the seams in the directions indicated. Sew the rows together; press the seams in the directions indicated.

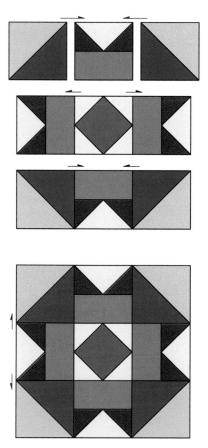

Stars over Mitford Block

8. Repeat steps 1–7 to make the required number of blocks for the quilt size you are making, using the diagrams below for alternate placement of the dark and medium fabrics if desired.

ASSEMBLING THE QUILT TOP

1. Refer to the quilt plan to arrange the blocks in horizontal rows on your design wall. Sew the blocks in each row together; press the seams in opposite directions from row to row. Sew the rows together; press the seams in one direction.

2. Refer to "Plain Borders" on page 18 to add the inner and outer borders to the quilt top.

FINISHING

1. Layer the quilt top with batting and backing; hand or machine baste the layers together (see page 20).

2. Quilt as desired, bind the edges, add a label, and enjoy your finished quilt.

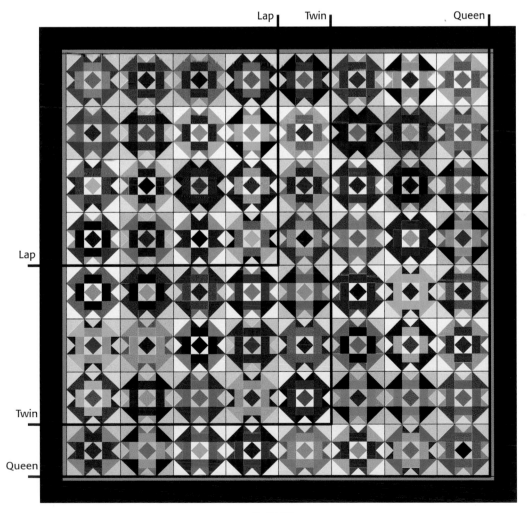

Quilt Plan

Butterfly Waltz

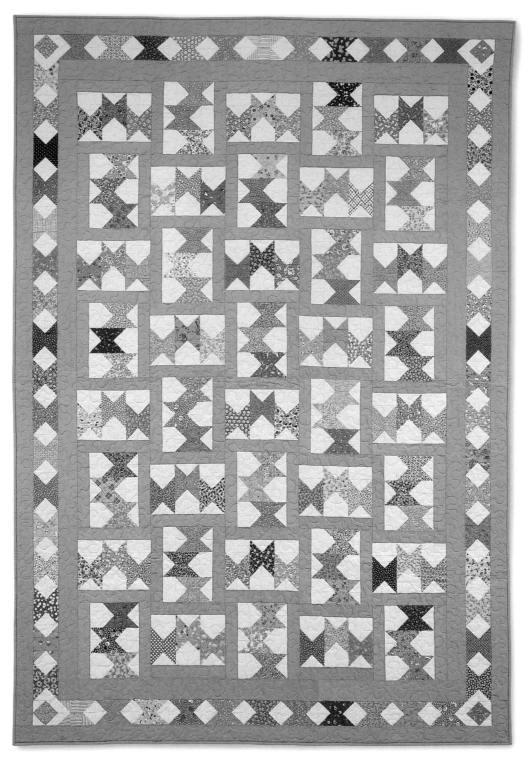

By Pat Speth, 70¼" x 101¾"

Finished block size: 10½"

～ Skill Level: Easy ～

While playing around with the small-wonders units, I came up with this delightful butterfly design. The sashing makes the blocks square, and giving every other block a quarter turn adds movement to this quilt. The vintage look was achieved with 1930s reproduction fabrics. Floral prints, Asian fabrics, or batiks would also be good choices for this quilt.

QUILT SIZES AND STATISTICS

	Lap	Twin	Queen
Size	59¾" x 59¾"	70¼" x 101¾"	101¾" x 101¾"
Number of blocks	16	40	64
Block set	4 x 4	5 x 8	8 x 8

MATERIALS

42"-wide fabric (40" of usable width after preshrinking and removing selvages)

	Lap	Twin	Queen
5" print squares	88	180	264
Background (light)	1¾ yards	3½ yards	5 yards
Sashing, borders, and binding	2⅜ yards	4¼ yards	5⅞ yards
Backing	3¾ yards	6⅛ yards	9 yards
Batting	64" x 64"	75" x 106"	106" x 106"

CUTTING

Cut all strips across the fabric width (crosswise grain).

NOTE: Wait to cut the strips for the inner border until the quilt top is finished (refer to "Pieced Borders" on page 19).

Lap Size

	First Cut		Second Cut	
	Number of Strips	Strip Width	Number of Pieces	Piece Size
Background	11	5"	88	5" x 5"
Sashing	11	2¼"	32	2¼" x 11"
Inner border	5	3⅛"		
Outer border	6	3"		
Binding	7	2½"		

Twin Size

	First Cut		Second Cut	
	Number of Strips	Strip Width	Number of Pieces	Piece Size
Background	23	5"	180	5" x 5"
Sashing	27	2¼"	80	2¼" x 11"
Inner border	8	3⅛"		
Outer border	9	3"		
Binding	10	2½"		

Queen Size

	First Cut		Second Cut	
	Number of Strips	Strip Width	Number of Pieces	Piece Size
Background	33	5"	264	5" x 5"
Sashing	43	2¼"	128	2¼" x 11"
Inner border	10	3⅛"		
Outer border	11	3"		
Binding	11	2½"		

MAKING THE BLOCKS

For each block, you will use:

- 3 print 5" squares
- 3 background 5" squares
- 2 sashing 2¼" x 11" strips

1. Refer to "Small-Wonders Units" on page 13 to sew one print and one background square together to make one pair of half-square-triangle units. Make three pairs of units for *each* block. Press the seams of each pair in opposite directions. Cut the half-square-triangle units into small-wonders units.

Half-Square-Triangle Units
Make 3 pairs of units for each block.

Small-Wonders Units

2. Arrange the small-wonders units from each half-square-triangle unit into four horizontal rows as shown, paying careful attention to the orientation of each half-square-triangle unit. Sew the units in each row together; press the seams in the directions indicated. Sew the rows together; press the seams in the directions indicated.

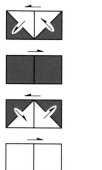

Butterfly Unit

3. *To make each block,* sew three units from step 2 together as shown, inverting the center unit. Press the seams in the directions indicated.

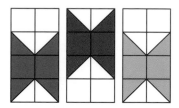

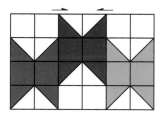

4. Stitch a sashing strip to the long edges of each block. Press the seams toward the sashing units.

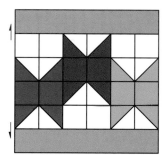

Butterfly Block

MAKING THE PIECED BORDER

Pieced-Border Units

	Lap	**Twin**	**Queen**
Side border units	9 per strip	17 per strip	17 per strip
Top and bottom border units	9 per strip	11 per strip	17 per strip
Total border units	36	56	68

1. Refer to "Small-Wonders Units" on page 13 to use print and background squares to make half-square-triangle units. Make one pair for *each* border unit

required. Cut the half-square-triangle units into small-wonders units. Discard or set aside the two background 2½" squares cut from each; you will not need them for this project.

2. For *each* border unit, arrange the remaining pieces from each small-wonders unit into three horizontal rows as shown. Sew the units in each row together; press the seams in the directions indicated. Sew the rows together; press the seams in the directions indicated.

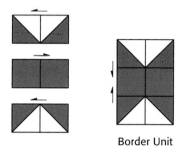

Border Unit

3. To make the corner units, trim four print squares to 4" x 4". Cut four background squares *each* into four 2¼" squares for a total of 16 squares. Draw a diagonal line on the wrong side of the 2¼" squares.

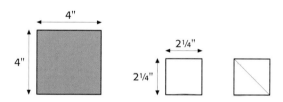

4. With right sides together, refer to "Sew and Flip" on page 16 to sew the 2¼" light squares to each corner of the 4" square, stitching opposite corners first. Trim and press each 2¼" square as shown.

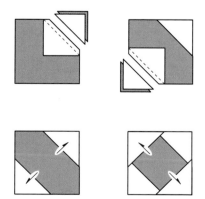

5. Stitch the required number of border units together to make each border strip. Stitch a corner unit to each end of the top and bottom borders. Press the seams in the directions indicated.

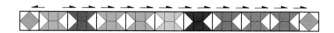

ASSEMBLING THE QUILT TOP

1. Refer to the quilt plan on page 74 to arrange the blocks in horizontal rows on your design wall, rotating every other block one-quarter turn to form the design.

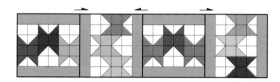

2. Stitch the blocks in each row together; press the seams in opposite directions from row to row. Sew the rows together; press the seams in one direction.

3. Refer to "Pieced Borders" on page 19 to add the inner, pieced, and outer borders to the quilt top.

FINISHING

1. Layer the quilt top with batting and backing; hand or machine baste the layers together (see page 20).

2. Quilt as desired, bind the edges, add a label, and enjoy your finished quilt.

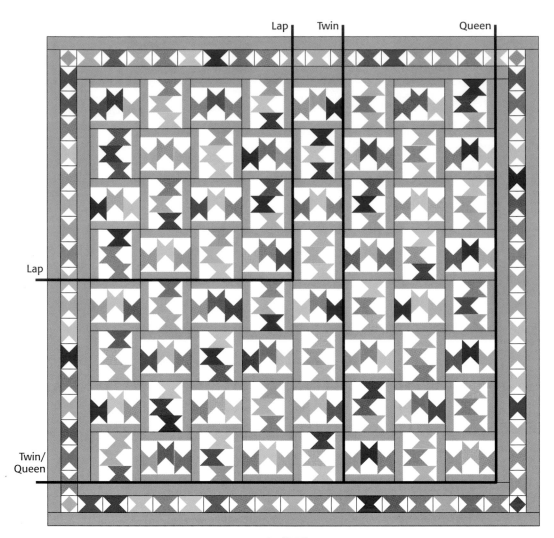

Quilt Plan

Rocky Road to Dublin

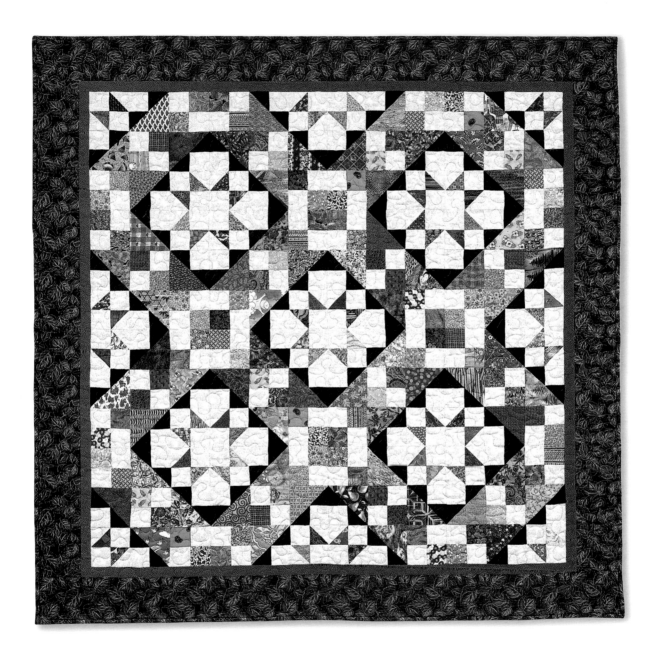

By Pat Speth, 59" x 59"

Finished block size: 12"

Four-patch, shaded-four-patch, and small half-square-triangle units are combined in this traditional block. The use of black tone-on-tone fabric in the small triangles of the shaded four-patch units emphasizes the secondary design created when the blocks are set together.

QUILT SIZES AND STATISTICS

	Lap	Twin	Queen
Size	59" x 59"	71" x 95"	107" x 107"
Number of blocks	16	35	64
Block set	4 x 4	5 x 7	8 x 8

MATERIALS

42"-wide fabric (40" of usable width after preshrinking and removing selvages)

	Lap	Twin	Queen
5" dark squares	72	158	288
Background (light)	1½ yards	3¼ yards	5½ yards
Black	⅝ yard	1⅛ yards	1⅞ yards
Inner border	⅜ yard	½ yard	⅝ yard
Outer border and binding	1½ yards	2 yards	2½ yards
Backing	3¾ yards	5¾ yards	9½ yards
Batting	63" x 63"	75" x 99"	111" x 111"

CUTTING

Cut all strips across the fabric width (crosswise grain).

Lap Size

	First Cut		Second Cut	
	Number of Strips	Strip Width	Number of Pieces	Piece Size
Background	3	5"	24	5" x 5"
	12	2½"	192	2½" x 2½"
Black	5	2⅞"	64	2⅞" x 2⅞" ◻*
Inner border	6	1½"		
Outer border	6	4¾"		
Binding	7	2½"		

Twin Size

	First Cut		Second Cut	
	Number of Strips	Strip Width	Number of Pieces	Piece Size
Background	7	5"	53	5" x 5"
	27	2½"	420	2½" x 2½"
Black	11	2⅞"	140	2⅞" x 2⅞" ◻*
Inner border	8	1½"		
Outer border	9	4¾"		
Binding	9	2½"		

Queen Size

	First Cut		Second Cut	
	Number of Strips	Strip Width	Number of Pieces	Piece Size
Background	12	5"	96	5" x 5"
	48	2½"	768	2½" x 2½"
Black	20	2⅞"	256	2⅞" x 2⅞" ◻*
Inner border	10	1½"		
Outer border	11	4¾"		
Binding	12	2½"		

◻ Cut each square in half once diagonally.

MAKING THE BLOCKS

For each block, you will use:

- 4½ dark 5" squares
- 1½ background 5" squares
- 12 background 2½" squares
- 8 black triangles

1. Refer to "Four-Patch Units" on page 11 to sew dark and background 5" squares together to make four-patch units. Make three four-patch units for *each* block required.

**Make 3
for each block.**

2. For *each* block, trim two dark 5" squares to 4⅞" x 4⅞". Cut each square in half once diagonally. Each square will yield two triangles.

3. Stitch a black triangle to two adjacent sides of a 2½" square of background fabric as shown. Press the seams toward the triangles. Stitch a dark triangle from step 2 to the long edge of the pieced triangle unit. Press the seam toward the large triangle. Make four units for each block.

**Make 4
for each block.**

4. For *each* block, cut one dark 5" square in half lengthwise and crosswise. Each square will yield four 2½" squares.

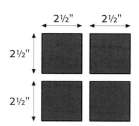

5. Draw a diagonal line on the wrong side of as many 2½" background squares as you have dark 2½" squares from step 4. Place the dark and background squares right sides together. Refer to "Sew and Flip" on page 16 to stitch the squares together. Trim and press each square as shown.

6. Stitch each unit from step 5 to a background 2½" square. Press the seam toward the pieced square. Stitch two units together as shown. Press the seam in the direction indicated. Make two units for each block.

**Make 2
for each block.**

7. *To make each block*, arrange three four-patch units from step 1, four units from step 3, and two units from step 6 into three horizontal rows as shown. Sew the units in each row together; press the seams in the directions indicated. Sew the rows together; press the seams in the direction indicated.

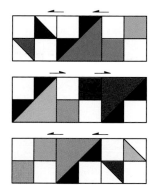 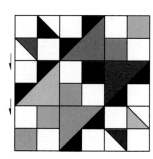

Rocky Road to Dublin Block

ASSEMBLING THE QUILT TOP

1. Refer to the quilt plan to arrange the blocks in horizontal rows on your design wall, rotating every other block one-quarter turn to form the design.

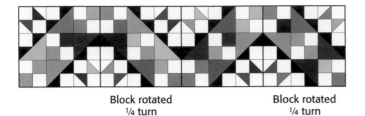

Block rotated
¼ turn

Block rotated
¼ turn

2. Sew the blocks in each row together; press the seams in opposite directions from row to row. Sew the rows together; press the seams in one direction.

3. Refer to "Plain Borders" on page 18 to add the inner and outer borders to the quilt top.

FINISHING

1. Layer the quilt top with batting and backing; hand or machine baste the layers together (see page 20).

2. Quilt as desired, bind the edges, add a label, and enjoy your finished quilt.

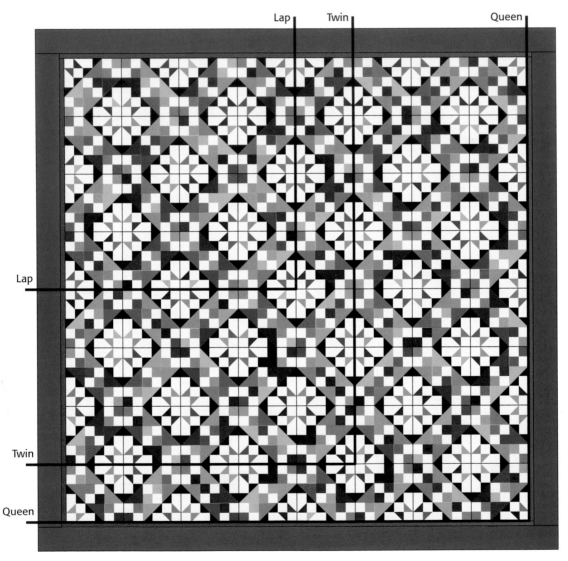

Quilt Plan

Blackford's Beauty

By Pat Speth and Roxie Speth, 59" x 59"

Finished block size: 16"

My daughter, Roxie, and I chose a rustic look for this quilt by selecting medium to dark prints and plaids along with assorted light background fabrics. Four-patch, picket-fence, and flying-geese units are put to good use in this fabulous block.

QUILT SIZES AND STATISTICS

	Lap	Twin	Queen
Size	59" x 59"	75" x 91"	107" x 107"
Number of blocks	9	20	36
Block set	3 x 3	4 x 5	6 x 6

MATERIALS

42"-wide fabric (40" of usable width after preshrinking and removing selvages)

	Lap	Twin	Queen
5" dark squares	9 pairs	20 pairs	36 pairs
	63 singles	140 singles	252 singles
5" light squares	99	220	396
Inner border	⅜ yard	½ yard	⅝ yard
Outer border and binding	1½ yards	2⅛ yards	2⅝ yards
Backing	3¾ yards	5½ yards	9½ yards
Batting	63" x 63"	79" x 95"	111" x 111"

CUTTING

Cut all strips across the fabric width (crosswise grain).

Lap Size

	Number of Strips	Strip Width
Inner border	6	1½"
Outer border	6	4¾"
Binding	7	2½"

Twin Size

	Number of Strips	Strip Width
Inner border	9	1½"
Outer border	9	4¾"
Binding	9	2½"

Queen Size

	Number of Strips	Strip Width
Inner border	10	1½"
Outer border	11	4¾"
Binding	12	2½"

MAKING THE BLOCKS

For each block, you will use:

- 9 single light 5" squares
- 7 single dark 5" squares
- 1 pair of light 5" squares
- 1 pair of dark 5" squares

1. Refer to "Four-Patch Units" on page 11 to sew single light and dark 5" squares together to make four-patch units. Make four for *each* block.

Make 4
for each block.

2. For *each* block, cut one pair and two single light 5" squares in half lengthwise and crosswise. Each square will yield four 2½" squares. You will use the eight matching squares in the flying-geese units and the rest in the picket-fence units.

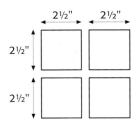

3. Refer to "Flying-Geese Units" on page 17 to cut one pair of dark 5" squares into four 2½" x 4½" rectangles for *each* block. Using eight matching 2½" squares from step 2, make the flying-geese units. Make four matching flying-geese units for *each* block.

Make 4
for each block.

4. Refer to "Picket-Fence Units" on page 15 to trim and cut four single dark 5" squares into 2½" x 4½" rectangles for *each* block. Using two matching light squares from step 2 for each pair of rectangles, make the picket-fence units as shown. Press the seams of each pair in opposite directions. Stitch the two rectangles in each pair together as shown. Make four units for *each* block.

Make 4
for each block.

5. Sew a flying-geese unit to each picket-fence unit as shown. Press the seam toward the flying-geese unit.

6. For *each* block, trim ½" from one edge of four light 5" squares. Cut the trimmed pieces in half in the opposite direction of the first cut as shown to yield eight 2½" x 4½" rectangles.

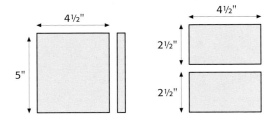

7. For *each* block, cut a dark 5" square in half lengthwise and crosswise to yield four 2½" squares.

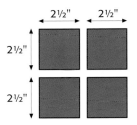

8. Arrange one four-patch unit from step 1, two light rectangles from step 6, and one dark square from step 7 into two horizontal rows as shown. Stitch the pieces in each row together. Press the seams in the directions indicated. Sew the rows together. Press the seam toward the four-patch unit. Make four units for *each* block.

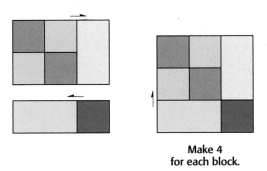

Make 4
for each block.

9. Trim the remaining light squares to 4½" x 4½".

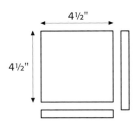

10. *To make each block*, arrange four matching units from step 5, four units from step 8, and one light 4½" square into three horizontal rows as shown. Sew the pieces in each row together; press the seams in the directions indicated. Sew the rows together to complete the block; press the seams in the directions indicated.

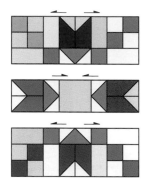

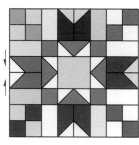

Blackford's Beauty Block

ASSEMBLING THE QUILT TOP

1. Refer to the quilt plan to arrange the blocks in horizontal rows on your design wall. Sew the blocks in each row together; press the seams in opposite directions from row to row. Sew the rows together; press the seams in one direction.

2. Refer to "Plain Borders" on page 18 to add the inner and outer borders to the quilt top.

FINISHING

1. Layer the quilt top with batting and backing; hand or machine baste the layers together (see page 20).

2. Quilt as desired, bind the edges, add a label, and enjoy your finished quilt.

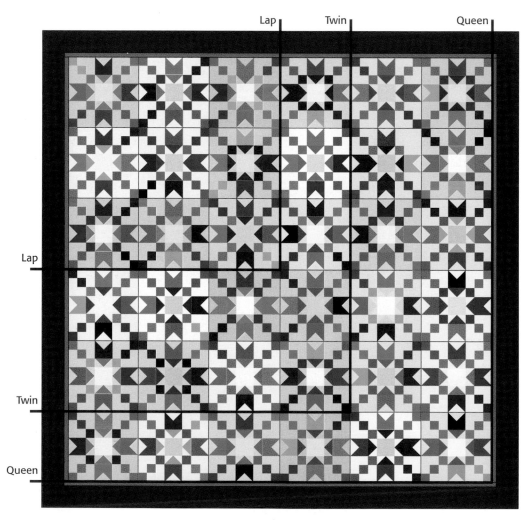

Quilt Plan

Sugar Bowl

By Pat Speth, 69¾" x 99¾"

Finished block size: 7½"

◦ Skill Level: Intermediate ◦

This traditional block uses left-sided and right-sided combination units to make the blocks and pieced border. I made my blocks with pastel prints in light and medium values, tossing in a dark now and then to add sparkle. A sashing strip made from border fabric and a floral print separates the rows.

Please note that the first two squares that are sewn together are the small triangles in the Sugar Bowl block. The third square that is added to the unit will be the larger triangle.

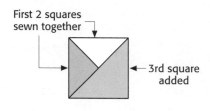

First 2 squares sewn together → 3rd square added

QUILT SIZES AND STATISTICS

	Lap	Twin	Queen
Size	54¾" x 62¼"	69¾" x 99¾"	100¼" x 104"
Number of blocks	25	63	99
Block set	5 x 5	7 x 9	11 x 9

MATERIALS

42"-wide fabric (40" of usable width after preshrinking and removing selvages)

	Lap	Twin	Queen
5" print squares	113	248	370
Background (light)	⅞ yard	1¾ yards	2½ yards
Sashing (light)	¼ yard	½ yard	⅝ yard
Sashing, borders, and binding (dark)	2 yards	3 yards	4¼ yards
Backing	3½ yards	6 yards	8⅞ yards
Batting	59" x 67"	74" x 104"	105" x 108"

CUTTING

Cut all strips across the fabric width (crosswise grain).

NOTE: Wait to cut the strips for the inner border until the quilt top is finished (refer to "Pieced Borders" on page 19).

Lap Size

	First Cut		Second Cut	
	Number of Strips	Strip Width	Number of Pieces	Piece Size
Background	5	5"	39	5" x 5"
Sashing (light)	4	1"		
Sashing (dark)	8	1¼"		
Inner border (sides)	3	2⅜"		
Inner border (top/bottom)	3	2⅛"		
Outer border	6	3¼"		
Binding	7	2½"		

Twin Size

	First Cut		Second Cut	
	Number of Strips	Strip Width	Number of Pieces	Piece Size
Background	11	5"	84	5" x 5"
Sashing (light)	11	1"		
Sashing (dark)	22	1¼"		
Inner border (sides)	5	2⅜"		
Inner border (top/bottom)	3	1⅞"		
Outer border	9	3¼"		
Binding	10	2½"		

Queen Size

	First Cut		Second Cut	
	Number of Strips	Strip Width	Number of Pieces	Piece Size
Background	16	5"	125	5" x 5"
Sashing (light)	17	1"		
Sashing (dark)	34	1¼"		
Inner border (sides)	5	2⅜"		
Inner border (top/bottom)	5	3¾"		
Outer border	11	3½"		
Binding	11	2½"		

MAKING THE BLOCKS

For each block, you will use:

- 3 print 5" squares
- 1 background 5" square

1. Refer to "Combination Units" on page 13 to sew one print and one background square together to make two half-square-triangle units. Center each unit on a print square and make the combination units. *Do not trim or press the units.* Make two different pairs of combination units for *each* block. When you have the required number of combination units made for the quilt top, decide the placement of the units in each block and press the seams in the directions indicated. Trim the units.

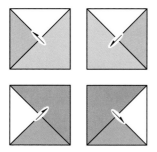

2. *To make each block,* arrange the pairs of previously determined units from step 1 into two vertical rows as shown. Sew the units in each row together; press the seams in the directions indicated. Sew the rows together; press the seams in the directions indicated.

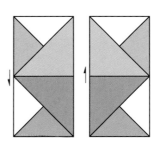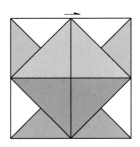

Sugar Bowl Block

MAKING THE PIECED BORDER

Pieced-Border Units

	Lap	Twin	Queen
Side border units	6 pairs + 1 single per strip	11 pairs + 1 single per strip	12 pairs per strip
Top and bottom border units	5 pairs + 1 single per strip	7 pairs + 1 single per strip	11 pairs + 1 single per strip
Total border units	22 pairs + 4 singles	36 pairs + 4 singles	46 pairs + 2 singles

1. Refer to step 1 of "Making the Blocks" at left to use print and background 5" squares to make the required number of combination units for the quilt size you are making. One pair of border units is equal to the right-sided and left-sided unit yielded from each combination unit.

2. Stitch the right-sided and left-sided units yielded from each combination unit together as shown until you have the amount of pairs needed for each border unit; press the seams in the direction indicated.

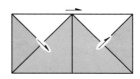

3. Refer to "Half-Square-Triangle Units" on page 12 to use 5" print and background squares to make four half-square-triangle units; trim the units to 4¼" x 4¼".

4. Refer to the quilt plan to assemble the required number of combination pairs for each border strip, adding a single unit to the end as shown when required.

Add a single combination unit to border strips when needed.

5. Stitch a half-square-triangle unit to each end of the top and bottom borders.

ASSEMBLING THE QUILT TOP

1. Stitch the light sashing strips together end to end to make one long strip. Stitch half of the dark sashing strips together in the same manner. Repeat with the remaining half of the dark sashing strips. Stitch the light and dark sashing strips together as shown to make a strip set.

2. Refer to the quilt plan to arrange the blocks in horizontal rows on a design wall. Stitch the blocks in each row together. Press the seams in one direction.

3. Measure the length of the block rows to determine the length to cut the sashing strips. Refer to the quilt plan to cut the number of sashing strips required for the quilt size you are making.

4. Use a pencil to mark the wrong side of the sashing strip in increments to line up with the blocks. The first and last marks will be 7¾" from the edge and the remaining marks will be 7½" apart.

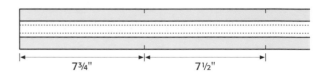

5. Alternately sew the block rows and the sashing strips together, lining up the pencil marks with the block seams; press the seams toward the sashing strips.

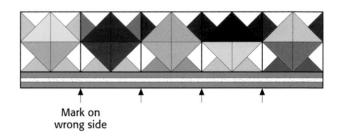

Mark on wrong side

6. Refer to "Pieced Borders" on page 19 to add the inner, pieced, and outer borders to the quilt top.

FINISHING

1. Layer the quilt top with batting and backing; hand or machine baste the layers together (see page 20).

2. Quilt as desired, bind the edges, add a label, and enjoy your finished quilt.

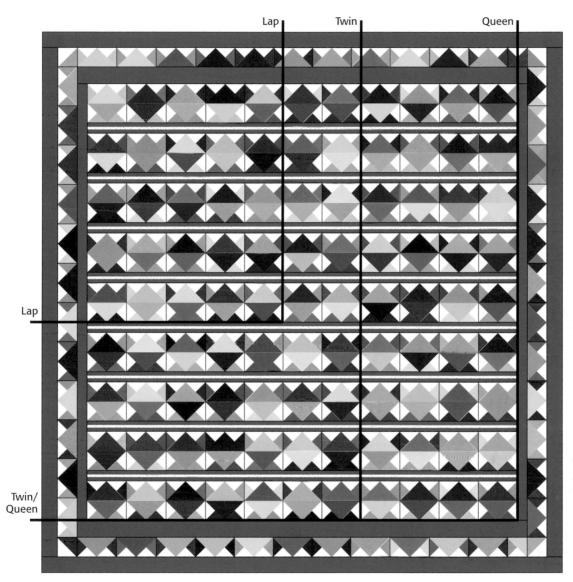

Quilt Plan

Brave World

By Pat Speth, 64½" x 64½"

Finished block size: 8"

~ Skill Level: Intermediate ~

I chose a very scrappy theme for this quilt by using an assortment of floral, geometric, tone-on-tone, and novelty prints, but it would look great in any fabric combination. The shaded four-patch unit, which is used in the block, is repeated in the pieced border.

QUILT SIZES AND STATISTICS

	Lap	Full	Queen
Size	64½" x 64½"	84½" x 104½"	104½" x 104½"
Number of blocks	25	63	81
Block set	5 x 5	7 x 9	9 x 9

MATERIALS

42"-wide fabric (40" of usable width after preshrinking and removing selvages)

	Lap	Full	Queen
5" dark squares	118	263	328
Background (light)	2 yards	4½ yards	5½ yards
Borders and binding	1¾ yards	2½ yards	2⅝ yards
Backing	4 yards	7½ yards	9¼ yards
Batting	69" x 69"	89" x 109"	109" x 109"

CUTTING

Cut all strips across the fabric width (crosswise grain).

Lap Size

	First Cut		Second Cut	
	Number of Strips	Strip Width	Number of Pieces	Piece Size
Background	10	2½"	40	2½" x 8½"
	12	2⅞"	152	2⅞" x 2⅞" ◻*
Inner border	6	2½"		
Outer border	8	2½"		
Binding	7	2½"		

Full Size

	First Cut		Second Cut	
	Number of Strips	Strip Width	Number of Pieces	Piece Size
Background	28	2½"	110	2½" x 8½"
	26	2⅞"	334	2⅞" x 2⅞" ◻*
Inner border	9	2½"		
Outer border	11	2½"		
Binding	11	2½"		

Queen Size

	First Cut		Second Cut	
	Number of Strips	Strip Width	Number of Pieces	Piece Size
Background	36	2½"	144	2½" x 8½"
	32	2⅞"	416	2⅞" x 2⅞" ◻*
Inner border	10	2½"		
Outer border	12	2½"		
Binding	12	2½"		

* ◻ Cut each square in half once diagonally.

MAKING THE BLOCKS

For each block, you will use:

- 3 dark 5" squares
- 8 background triangles

1. For *each* block, trim two dark 5" squares to measure 4⅞" x 4⅞". Cut each square in half once diagonally. Each square will yield two triangles.

2. Divide the number of blocks required by four and round up to the nearest whole number. Cut that number of dark 5" squares in half lengthwise and crosswise. Each square will yield four 2½" squares.

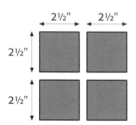

3. Stitch a 2⅞" background triangle to two adjacent sides of a dark 2½" square from step 2. Press the seams toward the triangles. Stitch a dark 4⅞" triangle from step 1 to the long edge of the pieced triangle unit. Press the seam toward the large triangle. Make four shaded four-patch units for *each* block.

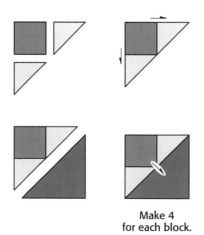

Make 4
for each block.

4. *To make each block,* arrange four shaded four-patch units into two horizontal rows as shown. Sew the units in each row together; press the seams in the directions indicated. Sew the rows together; press the seam in the direction indicated.

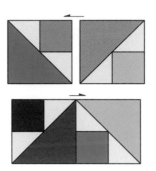

Brave World Block

ASSEMBLING THE QUILT TOP

1. Refer to the quilt plan on page 92 to determine the number of sashing squares needed; divide this number by four. Cut that number of dark 5" squares in half lengthwise and crosswise. Each square will yield four 2½" squares for the sashing. For more variety, combine these squares with any leftover 2½" squares from the shaded four-patch units.

2. Refer to the quilt plan to alternately arrange the blocks and 2½" x 8½" background strips on your design wall as shown to make the block rows. Alternately arrange the background strips and sashing squares to make the sashing rows. Sew the pieces in each row together; press the seams toward the background strips. Sew the rows together; press the seams toward the sashing rows.

Block
row

Sashing
row

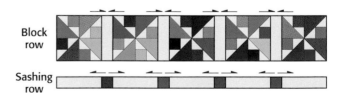

MAKING THE PIECED BORDER

Pieced-Border Units

	Lap	Full	Queen
Side border units	12 per strip	22 per strip	22 per strip
Top and bottom border units	12 per strip	17 per strip	22 per strip
Corner units	4	4	4
Total border units	52	82	92

1. Follow steps 1–3 of "Making the Blocks" on page 90 to make the required number of shaded four-patch border units for the quilt size you are making. One shaded four-patch unit is equal to one border unit.

2. Sew the required number of border units together as shown to make each strip; press the seams in one direction.

3. Refer to "Pieced Borders" on page 19 to measure, cut, and stitch an inner-border strip to each pieced side border as shown; press the seam toward the inner border. Sew the combined side borders to the quilt top; press the seam toward the inner border.

Side Pieced-Border Strip

4. From an inner-border strip, cut four spacer strips, 2½" x 4½". Sew a spacer strip to each end of the top and bottom pieced-border strips. Add a shaded four-patch unit to each end of the top and bottom pieced-border strips as shown. Press the seams toward the spacer strips.

5. Add an inner-border strip to each top and bottom pieced-border strip in the same manner as you did for the side pieced-border strips. Sew the combined top and bottom borders to the quilt top; press the seams toward the inner border.

Top and Bottom Pieced Border

6. Refer to "Plain Borders" on page 18 to add the outer border to the quilt top.

FINISHING

1. Layer the quilt top with batting and backing; hand or machine baste the layers together (see page 20).

2. Quilt as desired, bind the edges, add a label, and enjoy your finished quilt.

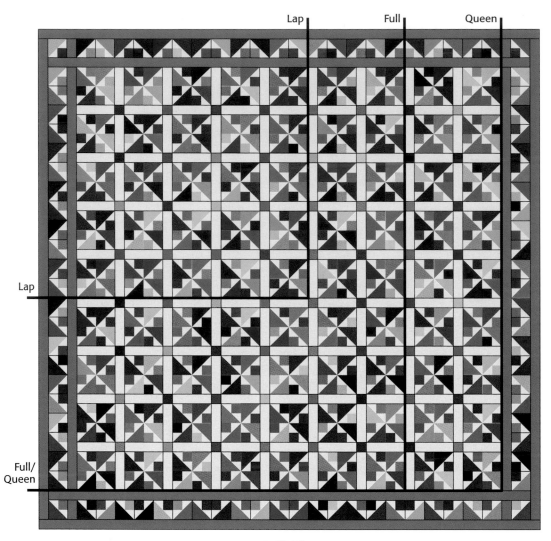

Quilt Plan

Mystery Flower Garden

By Pat Speth, 70" x 91"

Finished block size: 10½"

~ Skill Level: Intermediate ~

The hourglass unit and a version of the combination unit team up to make this wonderful quilt. Using 5" squares in a variety of colors and in light, medium, and dark values creates sparkle. The hourglass unit is again put to great use in the delightful border.

QUILT SIZES AND STATISTICS

	Lap	Twin	Queen
Size	59½" x 59½"	70" x 91"	101½" x 101½"
Number of blocks	16	35	64
Block set	4 x 4	5 x 7	8 x 8

MATERIALS

42"-wide fabric (40" of usable width after preshrinking and removing selvages)

	Lap	Twin	Queen
5" dark squares	92	180	308
Background (light)	2⅛ yards	3⅞ yards	6⅛ yards
Borders and binding	1⅝ yards	2¼ yards	2⅞ yards
Backing	3¾ yards	5½ yards	9 yards
Batting	64" x 64"	74" x 95"	106" x 106"

CUTTING

Cut all strips across the fabric width (crosswise grain).

NOTE: Wait to cut the strips for the inner border until the quilt top is finished (refer to "Pieced Borders" on page 19).

Lap Size

	First Cut		Second Cut	
	Number of Strips	Strip Width	Number of Pieces	Piece Size
Background	8	5"	60	5" x 5"
	4	4½"	32	4½" x 4½"
	2	4"	16	4" x 4"
Inner border	5	2¼"		
Outer border	6	3¾"		
Binding	7	2½"		

Twin Size

	First Cut		Second Cut	
	Number of Strips	Strip Width	Number of Pieces	Piece Size
Background	14	5"	110	5" x 5"
	9	4½"	70	4½" x 4½"
	4	4"	35	4" x 4"
Inner border	7	2¼"		
Outer border	9	3¾"		
Binding	9	2½"		

Queen Size

	First Cut		Second Cut	
	Number of Strips	Strip Width	Number of Pieces	Piece Size
Background	23	5"	180	5" x 5"
	16	4½"	128	4½" x 4½"
	7	4"	64	4" x 4"
Inner border	10	2¼"		
Outer border	11	3¾"		
Binding	11	2½"		

MAKING THE BLOCKS

For each block, you will use:

- 4 dark 5" squares
- 2 background 5" squares
- 2 background 4½" squares
- 1 background 4" square

1. Refer to "Hourglass Units" on page 14 to sew dark and background 5" squares together to make half-square-triangle units. Sew two different half-square-triangle units together to make hourglass units. Make four matching hourglass units for *each* block.

Make 4
for each block.

2. Refer to steps 1–4 of "Half-Square-Triangle Units" on page 12 to sew two different dark 5" squares together to make half-square-triangle units. *Do not trim the units.* Make two units for *each* block.

3. For *each* half-square-triangle unit made in step 2, draw a diagonal line on the wrong side of a background 4½" square. With right sides together, center the background square on top of each half-square-triangle unit. Notice the direction of the drawn line in relation to the seams of the half-square-triangle unit. (The background square will be slightly smaller than the half-square-triangle unit.) Stitch a "slim" ¼"-wide seam on both sides of the diagonal line.

4. Cut the squares apart on the diagonal line. Set the stitching and press the seam toward the large triangle.

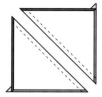

5. Align the 45° diagonal line of a square ruler with the long seam line in each unit. Position the ruler so that the fabric extends past the ruler on two adjacent edges, with the two remaining edges extending past the 4" lines of the ruler and with the 4" line meeting the short seam line on each unit. Trim away the fabric extending past the ruler.

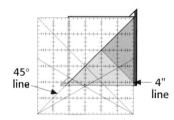 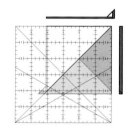

45°
line

4"
line

Trim excess.

6. Reposition each unit so that the two trimmed edges now line up with the 4" lines on the ruler and the 45° diagonal line of the ruler is aligned with the long seam line. Trim the remaining two edges. You should have a perfect, 4"-square combination unit. Make four for each block.

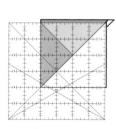 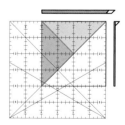

Trim excess.

4"

4"

Make 4
for each block.

7. *To make each block*, arrange four matching hourglass units, two right and two left combination units from the same fabrics, and one 4" background square into three horizontal rows as shown. Sew the units in each row together; press the seams in the directions indicated. Sew the rows; press the seams in the directions indicated.

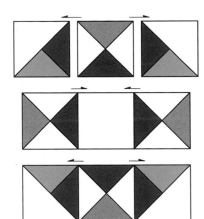

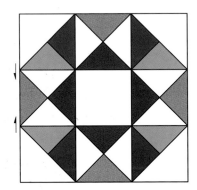

Mystery Flower Garden Block

MAKING THE PIECED BORDER

Pieced-Border Units

	Lap	Twin	Queen
Side border units	13 per strip	22 per strip	25 per strip
Top and bottom border units	15 per strip	18 per strip	27 per strip
Total border units	56	80	104

1. Refer to "Hourglass Units" on page 14 to sew the dark and background 5" squares together to make the required number of hourglass units for the quilt size you are making. Each hourglass unit equals one border unit.

2. Stitch the required number of hourglass units together as shown to make each border strip; press the seams in one direction.

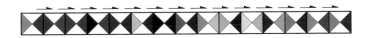

ASSEMBLING THE QUILT TOP

1. Refer to the quilt plan to arrange the blocks into horizontal rows on your design wall. Sew the blocks in each row together; press the seams in opposite directions from row to row. Sew the rows together; press the seams in one direction.

2. Refer to "Pieced Borders" on page 19 to add the inner, pieced, and outer borders to the quilt top.

FINISHING

1. Layer the quilt top with batting and backing; hand or machine baste the layers together (see page 20).

2. Quilt as desired, bind the edges, add a label, and enjoy your finished quilt.

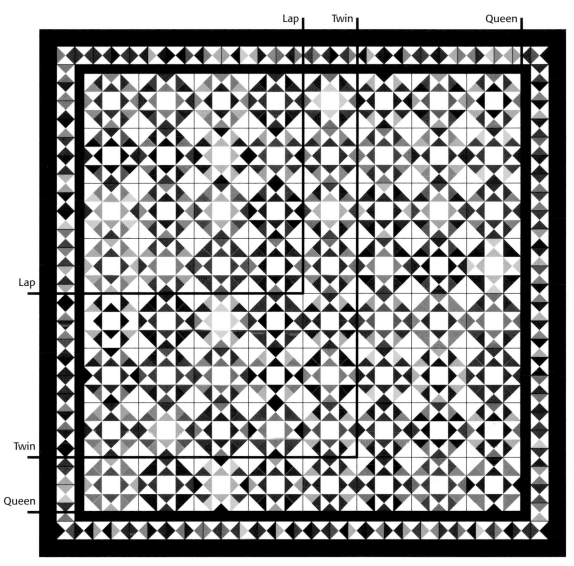

Quilt Plan

Dawn to Dusk

By Pat Speth, 78½" x 102½"

Finished block size: 6"

∽ Skill Level: Intermediate ∽

This quilt was inspired by a Sharyn Craig workshop that I attended. The Dawn to Dusk block is made from pairs of batik and background 5" squares, resulting in leftover rectangles of each. Because I hate to waste fabric, I designed the border to use up the leftover rectangles. The batik fabrics in the blocks reminded me of sunrises and sunsets, hence the name "Dawn to Dusk." You might enjoy making this quilt so much that you'll want to work on it from dawn to dusk!

QUILT SIZES AND STATISTICS

	Lap	Twin	Queen
Size	53" x 53"	78½" x 102½"	102½" x 102½"
Number of blocks	36	140	196
Block set	6 x 6	10 x 14	14 x 14

MATERIALS

42"-wide fabric (40" of usable width after preshrinking and removing selvages)

	Lap	Twin	Queen
5" dark squares	36 pairs 14 singles	140 pairs	196 pairs
5" light squares	36 pairs 16 singles	140 pairs 4 singles	196 pairs 4 singles
Borders and binding	1½ yards	2½ yards	2⅞ yards
Backing	3⅜ yards	7⅛ yards	9⅛ yards
Batting	57" x 57"	83" x 107"	107" x 107"

CUTTING

Cut all strips across the fabric width (crosswise grain).

NOTE: Wait to cut the strips for the inner border until the quilt top is finished (refer to "Pieced Borders" on page 19).

Lap Size

	Number of Strips	Strip Width
Inner border	5	2½"
Outer border	6	2¾"
Binding	6	2½"

Twin Size

	Number of Strips	Strip Width
Inner border	9	2½"
Outer border	9	3½"
Binding	10	2½"

Queen Size

	Number of Strips	Strip Width
Inner border	10	2½"
Outer border	11	3½"
Binding	11	2½"

MAKING THE BLOCKS

For each block, you will use:

- 1 pair of dark 5" squares
- 1 pair of light 5" squares

1. Select one dark pair of squares and one light pair of squares. Separate the pairs into sets A and B; use one dark and one light square in each set.

Set A

Set B

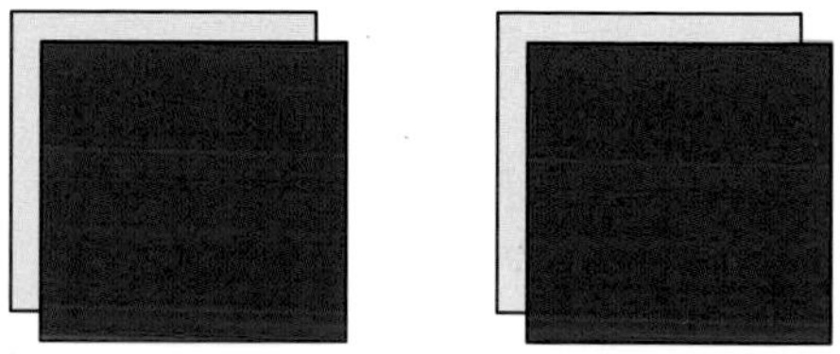

2. Cut the squares in set A in half as shown. Set aside one light and one dark rectangle for use in the border. Trim ½" from one end of the remaining light and dark rectangles.

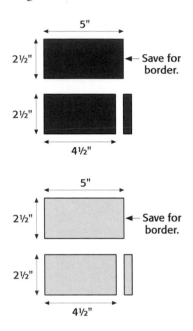

3. Cut the squares in set B in half lengthwise and crosswise. Each square will yield four 2½" squares.

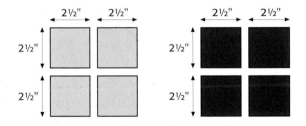

4. Draw a diagonal line on the wrong side of three light squares from step 3. Place each marked light square over a dark square from step 3, right sides together. Stitch, following the "Sew and Flip" method on page 16. Press the seams toward the dark triangles.

5. Arrange the units from steps 2–4 into three horizontal rows as shown. Sew the pieces in each row together; press the seams in the directions indicated. Sew the rows together; press the seams in the directions indicated.

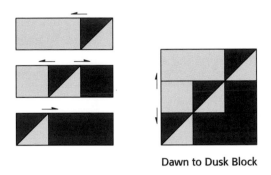

Dawn to Dusk Block

6. Repeat steps 1–5 to make the required number of blocks for the quilt size you are making.

MAKING THE PIECED BORDER

Pieced-Border Units

	Lap	Twin	Queen
Side border units	10 per strip	22 per strip	22 per strip
Top and bottom border units	10 per strip	16 per strip	22 per strip
Total border units	40	76	88

NOTE: For the lap-size quilt only, you will need to cut additional pieces from the single dark and light squares to make the required number of units.

1. From the rectangles that were set aside in step 1 of "Making the Blocks," select one light and one dark rectangle for each border unit required. Trim ½" from one end of each rectangle so that they measure 2½" x 4½". These will be used for the large part of each unit.

2. Again, going back to the rectangles that you set aside in step 1 of "Making the Blocks," divide the number of border units required by two and select that number of light rectangles and that number of dark rectangles. Cut each rectangle in half to yield two 2½" squares.

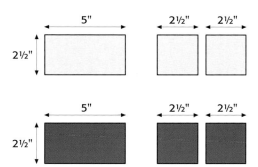

3. Draw a diagonal line on the wrong side of each of the 2½" squares.

4. Refer to "Picket-Fence Units" on page 15 to sew the dark 2½" squares to the light rectangles from step 1 as shown. Sew the light 2½" squares to the dark rectangles from step 1 as shown. Press the seams in the directions indicated.

Light Picket-Fence Unit

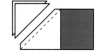

Dark Picket-Fence Unit

5. Sew each light picket-fence unit to a dark picket-fence unit as shown to make the required number of border units for the quilt size you are making.

Border Unit

6. For *each* of the four corner units, trim a light 5" square to 4½" x 4½". Cut two dark 2½" squares from the leftover rectangles.

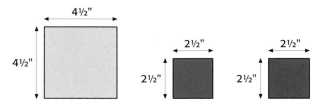

7. With right sides together, sew a dark 2½" square to opposite corners of each light 4½" square, referring to "Sew and Flip" on page 16. Trim and press each 2½" square as shown.

Corner Unit

8. Stitch the required number of border units together as shown to make each border, adding a corner unit to each end of the top and bottom borders.

Top and Bottom Border

ASSEMBLING THE QUILT TOP

1. Refer to the quilt plan on page 102 to arrange the blocks in horizontal rows on your design wall. Sew the blocks in each row together; press the seams in opposite directions from row to row. Sew the rows together; press the seams in one direction.

2. Refer to "Pieced Borders" on page 19 to add the inner, pieced, and outer borders to the quilt top.

FINISHING

1. Layer the quilt top with batting and backing; hand or machine baste the layers together (see page 20).

2. Quilt as desired, bind the edges, add a label, and enjoy your finished quilt.

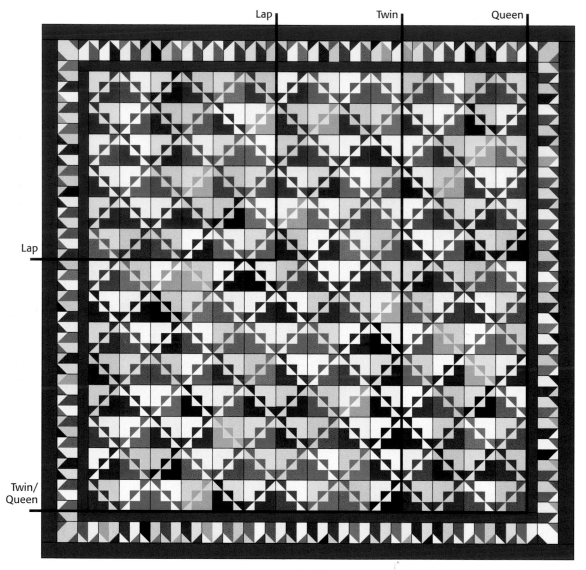

Quilt Plan

Texas Star

By Pat Speth, 52" x 64"

Finished block size: 10½"

Single 5" squares are used to construct this Texas Star block. I used 1800s reproduction fabrics and three squares from the same color family in each of the blocks. Flying-geese units are used in the pieced border to add to the traditional flavor of this quilt.

QUILT SIZES AND STATISTICS

	Lap	Twin	Queen
Size	52" x 64"	64" x 88"	100" x 100"
Number of blocks	12	24	49
Block set	3 x 4	4 x 6	7 x 7

MATERIALS

42"-wide fabric (40" of usable width after preshrinking and removing selvages)

	Lap	Twin	Queen
5" dark squares	86	140	239
Background	2⅛ yards	3½ yards	6¼ yards
Sashing	½ yard	1 yard	2 yards
Borders and binding	1⅞ yards	2 yards	2⅜ yards
Backing	3⅜ yards	5⅜ yards	8⅞ yards
Batting	56" x 68"	68" x 92"	104" x 104"

CUTTING

Cut all strips across the fabric width (crosswise grain).

NOTE: Wait to cut the strips for the inner border until the quilt top is finished (refer to "Pieced Borders" on page 19).

Lap Size

	First Cut		Second Cut	
	Number of Strips	Strip Width	Number of Pieces	Piece Size
Background	3	5"	24	5" x 5"
	5	4"	48	4" x 4"
	13	2½"	200	2½" x 2½"
			6	2¼" x 2¼"
Sashing	6	2¼"	17	2¼" x 11"
Inner border (sides)	3	3"		
Inner border (top/bottom)	3	2⅞"		
Outer border	7	2¼"		
Binding	7	2½"		

Twin Size

	First Cut		Second Cut	
	Number of Strips	Strip Width	Number of Pieces	Piece Size
Background	6	5"	48	5" x 5"
	10	4"	96	4" x 4"
	17	2½"	272	2½" x 2½"
	1	2¼"	15	2¼" x 2¼"
Sashing	13	2¼"	38	2¼" x 11"
Inner border (sides)	4	2⅞"		
Inner border (top/bottom)	3	2⅝"		
Outer border	9	2¼"		
Binding	9	2½"		

Queen Size

	First Cut		Second Cut	
	Number of Strips	Strip Width	Number of Pieces	Piece Size
Background	13	5"	98	5" x 5"
	20	4"	196	4" x 4"
	23	2½"	368	2½" x 2½"
	3	2¼"	36	2¼" x 2¼"
Sashing	28	2¼"	84	2¼" x 11"
Inner border	10	2½"		
Outer border	10	2¼"		
Binding	11	2½"		

MAKING THE BLOCKS

For each block, you will use:

- 3 dark 5" squares
- 2 background 5" squares
- 4 background 4" squares

1. Refer to "Hourglass Units" on page 14 to sew dark and background 5" squares together to make hourglass units. One dark and one background square will make two matching hourglass units. Make two sets of two matching hourglass units for each block.

Make 4
for each block.

2. For *each* block, trim a dark 5" square to 4" square.

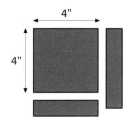

3. *To make each block*, arrange four identical hourglass units, four background 4" squares, and one dark 4" square into three horizontal rows as shown. Sew the units in each row together; press the seams in the directions indicated. Sew the rows together; press the seams in the directions indicated.

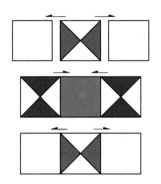

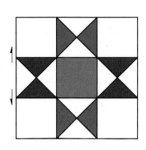

Texas Star Block

MAKING THE PIECED BORDER

Pieced-Border Units

	Lap	Twin	Queen
Side border units	13 per strip	19 per strip	22 per strip
Top and bottom border units	12 per strip	15 per strip	24 per strip
Total border units	50	68	92

1. Refer to "Flying-Geese Units" on page 17 to use the remaining dark 5" squares and the background 2½" squares to make flying-geese units. You will need two flying-geese units for each border unit required.

2. Sew the flying-geese units together in pairs as shown to make each border unit. Wait to press the center seam until you have them arranged into border strips.

3. Arrange the required number of flying-geese units as shown to make each border strip; press the center seam of the units in opposite directions. Stitch the units together; press the seams in one direction.

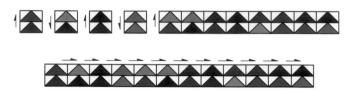

ASSEMBLING THE QUILT TOP

1. Refer to the quilt plan to alternately arrange the blocks and 2¼" x 11" sashing strips on a design wall as shown to make the block rows. Alternately arrange the sashing strips and 2¼" background squares to make the sashing rows. Sew the pieces in each row together; press the seams toward the

sashing strips. Sew the rows together; press the seams toward the sashing rows.

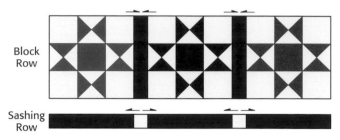

Block Row

Sashing Row

2. Refer to "Pieced Borders" on page 19 to add the inner, pieced, and outer borders to the quilt top.

FINISHING

1. Layer the quilt top with batting and backing; hand or machine baste the layers together (see page 20).

2. Quilt as desired, bind the edges, add a label, and enjoy your finished quilt.

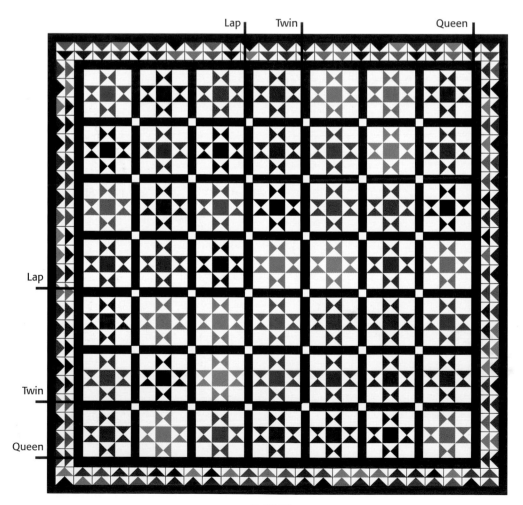

Lap Twin Queen

Lap

Twin

Queen

Quilt Plan

Churn Dash

By Pat Speth, 73" x 101"

Finished block size: 10"

◞ *Skill Level: Intermediate* ◞

The Churn Dash block is actually easy to make, but I've given this quilt an intermediate skill rating because of the diagonal set and pieced border, which add visual interest to this quilt. You may want to wait until after you stitch the blocks together before you select the fabrics for the setting triangles and outer border.

QUILT SIZES AND STATISTICS

	Lap	Twin	Queen
Size	57" x 57"	73" x 101"	101" x 101"
Number of blocks	13	39	61
Diagonal block set	3 x 3	4 x 6	6 x 6

MATERIALS

42"-wide fabric (40" of usable width after preshrinking and removing selvages)

	Lap	Twin	Queen
5" dark squares	13 pairs	39 pairs	61 pairs
	24 singles	58 singles	84 singles
5" light squares	54	146	222
Setting triangles and inner border	1⅛ yards	1⅝ yards	2⅛ yards
Outer border and binding	1½ yards	2⅛ yards	2½ yards
Backing	3⅝ yards	6 yards	9 yards
Batting	61" x 61"	77" x 105"	105" x 105"

CUTTING

Cut all strips across the fabric width (crosswise grain).

Note: Wait to cut the strips for the inner border until the quilt top is finished (refer to "Pieced Borders" on page 19).

Lap Size

	First Cut		Second Cut	
	Number of Strips	Strip Width	Number of Pieces	Piece Size
Setting triangles	1	15⅜"	2	15⅜" x 15⅜"
	1	8"	2	8" x 8"
Inner border	6	1⅜"		
Outer border	6	4¾"		
Binding	7	2½"		

Twin Size

	First Cut		Second Cut	
	Number of Strips	Strip Width	Number of Pieces	Piece Size
Setting triangles	2	15⅜"	4	15⅜" x 15⅜"
			2	8" x 8"
Inner border (sides)	5	2⅜"		
Inner border (top/bottom)	4	2¼"		
Outer border	9	4¾"		
Binding	10	2½"		

Queen Size

	First Cut		Second Cut	
	Number of Strips	Strip Width	Number of Pieces	Piece Size
Setting triangles	3	15⅜"	5	15⅜" x 15⅜"
			2	8" x 8"
Inner border	10	2¼"		
Outer border	11	4¾"		
Binding	11	2½"		

MAKING THE BLOCKS

For each block, you will use:

- 1 pair of dark 5" squares
- 1 single dark 5" square
- 3¼ light 5" squares

1. Using one pair of dark 5" squares and two light 5" squares, refer to "Half-Square-Triangle Units" on page 12 to make half-square-triangle units. Make four units for *each* block.

Make 4
for each block.

2. Refer to "Two-Patch Units" on page 11 to sew dark and light 5" squares together to make small two-patch units. Make four for *each* block.

Make 4
for each block.

3. Divide the number of blocks needed by four and round up to the nearest whole number. Cut that amount of light 5" squares in half lengthwise and crosswise. Each square will yield four 2½" squares.

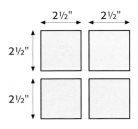

4. *To make each block*, arrange four half-square-triangle units with matching dark halves, four small two-patch units with matching dark halves

but a different dark than the half-square-triangle units, and one light 2½" square into three horizontal rows as shown. Sew the pieces in each row together; press the seams in the directions indicated. Sew the rows together; press the seams in the directions indicated.

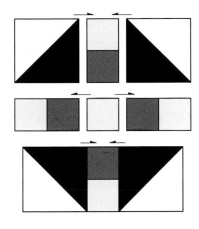

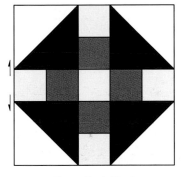

Churn Dash Block

MAKING THE PIECED BORDER

Pieced-Border Units

	Lap	Twin	Queen
Side border units	11 per strip	22 per strip	22 per strip
Top and bottom border units	11 per strip	16 per strip	23 per strip
Total border units	44	76	90

1. Refer to "Two-Patch Units" on page 11 to sew light and dark 5" squares together to make the required number of small two-patch units for the

quilt size you are making. Each two-patch unit equals one border unit.

2. Stitch the required number of small two-patch units together as shown to make each border strip. Press the seams in one direction.

ASSEMBLING THE QUILT TOP

1. Cut the 8" setting-triangle squares in half once diagonally to yield four corner triangles.

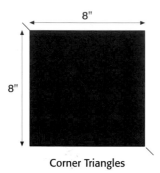

Corner Triangles

2. Cut the 15⅜" setting-triangle squares in half twice diagonally. Each square will yield four side setting triangles.

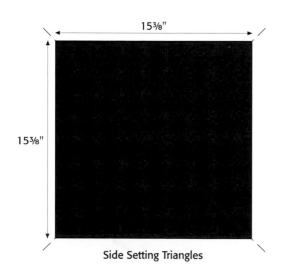

Side Setting Triangles

3. Refer to the quilt plan for the size you are making to arrange the blocks and setting triangles in diagonal rows on your design wall. Sew the pieces in each row together; press the seams in opposite directions from row to row. Sew the rows together; press the seams in one direction. Add the corner triangles last.

4. Using a ruler and rotary cutter, trim the excess from the setting triangles, leaving a ¼"-wide seam allowance beyond the block points.

5. Refer to "Pieced Borders" on page 19 to add the inner, pieced, and outer borders to the quilt top.

FINISHING

1. Layer the quilt top with batting and backing; hand or machine baste the layers together (see page 20).

2. Quilt as desired, bind the edges, add a label, and enjoy your finished quilt.

Lap-Size Quilt Plan

Twin-Size Quilt Plan

Queen-Size Quilt Plan

About the Author

Pat Speth began quilting in 1989 and has a special love for scrap quilts. She enjoys discovering traditional blocks and designing new ones that can be made from 5" squares. In July 2003, Pat began a full-time quilting career and enjoys traveling and teaching workshops. Pat and her husband, Dan, live in Iowa where you need two quilts on every bed in the winter. They have a son, Ray, and a daughter, Roxie, both in college. This is Pat's second book; her first book, *Nickel Quilts*, which she coauthored with Charlene Thode, was published in 2002. Visit Pat's Web site at www.patspeth.com.